MACDONALD ILLUSTRATED CLASSICS

GENERAL EDITOR: MALCOLM ELWIN

3

A Sentimental Journey

LAURENCE STERNE

A SENTIMENTAL JOURNEY

through France and Italy

BY Mr YORICK

with an introduction by John Cowper Powys
and illustrations by Brian Robb

MACDONALD:LONDON

First published in 1768
First published in this series in 1948
Third impression April 1954

Published by
Macdonald & Co. (Publishers) Ltd.,
16 Maddox Street
Made and printed in Great Britain by
Purnell and Sons, Ltd., Paulton
(Somerset) and London

INTRODUCTION

Whether to belong to a "county family" is an advantage or the reverse to a man of letters remains an open question. But considering that his great-grandfather—who was Master of Jesus College, Cambridge, under Charles the First, and was imprisoned by Cromwell for offering up to that monarch's cause the rich plate of the University—when rewarded by Charles the Second with the Archbishopric of York hesitated not to divide four landed estates among his personal offspring, it was a privilege that Laurence Sterne unquestionably possessed.

It was at Clonmel in Ireland, as the son of Lieutenant Roger Sterne and of Agnes the daughter of an army "Suttler" called Nuttall and the widow of a Captain Hebert, that Laurence was born into the mad world he loved so well, on the twenty-fourth of November 1713.

The extraordinary thing about Sterne is that though his mental stature is of so much less weight and his genius so much less majestical—light indeed as a falling leaf in comparison—he yet in some odd manner seems to belong —born out of time and like a child among grown men— to the portion of the Elysian fields frequented by Rabelais and Cervantes.

Under the homely chimneys of Shandy Hall, as much as beneath the towering battlements of Thelema, bubbles that magic cauldron the lightest drop from which enables us to defy discomfort, sickness, misfortune, misunderstanding and death, while it leaves in the mouth no other taste than the salt of indifference towards the gods and the milk of compassion towards men.

Dragged about from barracks to barracks, perpetually jolting over uneven roads, perpetually tossing over rough seas, this second child of a good-natured simple-minded father and an ungenteel, much-enduring, constantly pregnant mother, got naturally a somewhat catch-as-catch-can education.

One of the saddest, liveliest, honestest, shortest autobiographies ever compiled is contained in the brief document written by Sterne himself entitled: "Particulars relating to my family and self for my Lydia" and bequeathed to this adored only daughter, "in case hereafter she might have a curiosity, or a kinder motive to know them."

In this life of himself as "object," written by himself as "subject," Sterne paints for us a most engaging picture of the heroic and spirited Lieutenant who begat all these ill-starred children; only two of whom, Laurence and Catharine, had the luck, if such it be, to grow up.

"My father was run through the body by Captain Phillips, in a duel, the quarrel being about a goose; with much difficulty he survived—for he was sent to Jamaica, where he soon fell by the country fever, which took away his senses first, and made a child of him, and then, in a month or two, walking about continually without complaining, till the moment he sat down in an armchair, and breathed his last. . . . My father was a little smart man—active to the last degree, in all exercises—most patient of fatigue and disappointments, of which it pleased God to give him full measure—he was in his temper somewhat rapid and hasty—but of a kindly, sweet disposition, void of all design; and so innocent in his own intentions, that he suspected no one; so that you might have cheated him ten times in a day, if nine had not been sufficient for your purpose——"

In this same miniature autobiography our author gives a frank description of the conditions under which fate inducted him into holy orders, when, after an epoch in a school in Halifax where he wrote "Lau. Sterne" in monstrous great letters on a white-washed ceiling, and an epoch at Jesus, Cambridge, where he made friends with that honeysuckle rogue, Hall-Stevenson of "Crazy Castle," who introduced him to Rabelais, "I came," he tells us, "to York and my uncle got me the living of Sutton . . . but he quarrelled with me afterwards because I would not write paragraphs in the newspapers—though he was a party-man, I was not, and detested such dirty work. . . .

"By my wife's means I got the living of Stillington . . . and I remained near twenty years at Sutton, doing duty at both places—I had then very good health. Books, painting, fiddling, and shooting were my amusements. . . . In the year 1760 I took a house at York for your mother and yourself, and went up to London to publish my two first volumes of Shandy.

"In that year Lord Falconbridge presented me with the curacy of Coxwold—a sweet retirement in comparison of Sutton. In sixty-two I went to France before the peace was concluded, and you both followed me.—I left you both in France, and in two years after I went to Italy for the recovery of my health—and when I called upon you I tried to engage your mother to return to England with me—she and yourself are at length come—and I have had the inexpressible joy of seeing my girl everything I wished her." And to this the publisher of the old ten-volume edition of his works adds the significant words, "This was written about six months only before his death."

Sterne's final farewell to the world he so unconquerably enjoyed is expressed in two letters, the first of which is to his daughter Lydia, and the second to that pair of kind and loyal friends, probably the most simply satisfactory of *all* his friends, Commodore and Mrs. James, in whose house he used to meet his last and by far his most serious love, Mrs. Eliza Draper, the girl who was married to her elderly husband when she was a child.

To Mrs. James he writes: "My physician says I am better . . . God knows; for I feel myself sadly wrong, and shall, if I recover, be a long while of gaining strength. Before I have gone through half this letter, I must stop to rest my weak hand a dozen times. Mr. James was so good as to call upon me yesterday . . . Do, dear Mrs. James, entreat him to come to-morrow or next day, for perhaps I have not many days or hours to live. I want to ask a favour of him if I find myself worse, that I shall beg of you if in this wrestling I come off conqueror. My spirits are fled. It is a bad omen. Do not weep, my dear lady. Your tears are too precious to be shed for me. Bottle them up, and may the cork never be drawn. Dearest, kindest, gentlest, and best of women ! May health, peace, and happiness prove your handmaids. If I die, cherish the remembrance of me, and forget the follies which you so often condemned which my heart, not my head betrayed me into. Should my child, my Lydia, want a mother, may I hope you will, if she is left parentless, take her to your bosom ? You are the only woman on earth I can depend upon for such a benevolent action. I wrote to her a fortnight ago and told her what, I trust, she will find in you. Mr. James will be a father to her . . . commend me to him, as I now commend you to that Being who takes under his care the good and kind part of the world. Adieu, all grateful thanks to you and Mr. James—from your affectionate friend, L. Sterne."

It was only ten days after writing this that he died ; and a certain John Macdonald of Scotland, who was "a young fellow-clansman of John Crawfurd of Errol" and was in attendance on that gentleman at a grand dinner-party of the dying man's friends, including, among a sprinkling of dukes and earls, Mr. Garrick the actor, Mr. Hume the philosopher, and the faithful Commodore James, has in a book about his own adventures described Sterne's death in the following manner:

"About this time Mr. Sterne, the celebrated author, was taken ill at the silk-bag shop in Old Bond Street. He was sometimes called Tristram Shandy, and sometimes Yorick, a very great favourite of the gentlemen. One day my master had company to dinner. 'John,' said he, 'go and inquire how Mr. Sterne is to-day.' I went to Mr. Sterne's lodgings; the mistress opened the door. I enquired how he did. She told me to go to the nurse. I went into the room and he was just a-dying. I waited ten minutes; but in five he said, 'Now it is come.' He put up his hand as if to stop a blow, and died in a minute. The gentlemen were all very sorry and lamented him very much."

He was buried in the "new burying-ground near Tyburn" of the parish of St. George's, Hanover Square, and with no mourners save Mr. James and possibly Mr. Becket, one of his publishers. What happened to the soul he was so positive he possessed after this unceremonious interment is a question fitter for discussion by Walter Shandy than by us, but only two days later his corpse was stolen by body-snatchers and sold to the Professor of Anatomy at Cambridge, who, as he was dissecting it with his accustomed scientific detachment, was surprised to see one of his audience faint away in horror. Like Hamlet with the skull of Yorick this agitated student *had recognized the dead.*

Sterne was forty-six when he became an author, "exchanging," as he says, "the spade," since he had tried to increase his income by a little amateur farming, "for the pen." The first volumes of *Tristram Shandy* were printed in York before being sent to the London publisher Dodsley, whither the author himself followed them in 1760 to find himself famous at the start and every copy of those first books already sold.[1]

The dominant feminine element in Sterne's life was of course *in himself*; but with his wife Elizabeth, née Lumley, a not very distant cousin of the celebrated Mrs. Montague, and a person with generations of genteel Yorkshire blood in her veins, he had been as much in love as he could be with anyone when he was strong and young. As to their daughter Lydia, she was the darling of his heart and his devotion to her never wavered from her birth to his death. Never has a hoity-toity, high-spirited young lady had such an infatuated father. Sterne doted on her and so apparently did her mother. Lydia was one of those young women who remain charming, though spoilt.

After his wife and daughter, the lady-loves of his life were not, taking everything into consideration, as many as some of us, in these modern days, might have expected. Miss Kitty de Fourmantelle, a refined singer of ballads, with a mother to look after her and in no financial necessity, seems to be the "dear Jenny" to whom he so frequently refers in *Tristram Shandy*; and although in his letters to her there is only one—and that a rather doubtful one—reference to the possibility of his becoming a widower and of their sharing bed and board, and though even his less indulgent chroniclers think it extremely doubtful if his dalliance with her ever reached the point of venial, not to speak of mortal, sin, there is no question but that she had him—soul and senses—in delicious thrall, and that it was only after his meeting with Eliza, at the

[1] *A Sentimental Journey* was published in 1768.

house of Mr., or, as we ought rather to say, Commodore James, that "dear Jenny's" light, gay, intoxicating attraction yielded to a headier and more dangerous ensorcerizing.

Sterne's Eliza was the daughter of Mr. Whitehill, an official of the East India Company, and from a letter of hers to the sagacious Mrs. James, whom Sterne always treated with especial respect and with whom he never seems to have attempted to flirt, she expresses an intelligent and indignant rebelliousness against the limited opportunities for a liberal education offered to young women in those days.

Eliza herself had been married off to the middle-aged Mr. Draper, another of the Company's officials, when she was fourteen. Thus it is by no means surprising that after Sterne's death she fled from India and competed with his daughter Lydia in selling every scrap of his handwriting she possessed or could get hold of.

But Parson Yorick's love-affairs are not the only stick with which his nineteenth-century disparagers belabour him. The unfortunate fact that his mother, Agnes Sterne—with whom lived his only surviving sister Catharine—though as an officer's widow she had a pension as large as the imaginary fortune brought to her son by his genteel wife, and who moreover kept an Embroidery School in Ireland, arrived post-haste to share his supposed opulence just at the inauspicious moment when he had finally rebelled against the tyranny of that Cathedral-Miser his Uncle Jaques, was what set going the unfair tale, publicized by Byron and so deeply relished by Thackeray, that this bewailer of dead donkeys let his mother go to a vagrant's jail.

As a matter of fact in both his mother's case and his wife's case—not to speak of his sister's—to the end of his days Sterne was doing more for these extremely exacting women than most men would have done; and before it was over the women themselves appear to have admitted this and matters seem to have been satisfactorily settled.

A writer as original as Sterne, and original in so special a way, possesses just the kind of genius which lends itself to the most personal of personal attacks: nor do these attacks cease with the passing of time. Every influential classic—and Sterne, who started something as new and soul-disturbing in European nerves as Rousseau did in European politics, deserves this name—should be re-criticized and re-appreciated with every fresh generation.

A curious interest can be found in comparing these successive verdicts and reactions; and in Sterne's case this interest is unusually provocative. Thackeray's moral hatred of him, for instance, is rendered the more piquant because this great society-frequenter and society-scourge, this very snob of very snobs, this self-righteous mocker of hypocrisy, whose massive and industrious art carries genius as far as genius *can* be carried by a respectable imagination that conceals a conventional heart only a little deeper than within a conventional sleeve, was so flagrantly influenced by the man he derides and reproaches.

Moving forward however to the more purely Victorian age, we find Mr. H. D. Traill, in his "English Men of Letters" book on Sterne, published in 1882, complaining that "until the appearance of Mr. Percy Fitzgerald's two stout volumes some eighteen years ago" there was nothing worthy of being called a "Life of Sterne"—all was criticism rather than biography.

Well, there is no need to be a Communist to feel in the air in 1948 an atmospheric if not a materialistic *intimation* that when Mr. Traill in 1882 quotes from Mr. Fitzgerald "of eighteen years before" that gentleman's praise of the *Sentimental Journey* and his words about "the fragrance that belongs to this one book alone," not to speak of his application to Sterne's "Sèvres china medalions" of a cultured traveller's French, a good deal less colloquial than our author's, both he and the gentleman he quotes are reacting to Sterne's work in an interestingly different manner from the way in which a young ex-service man, of literary taste, would react to-day.

But there are those whose response to the *Sentimental Journey* would be still a response to these "vignettes" at their face value; a response to the "little maid in the bookseller's shop who put her little present *à part*, to the charming Greuze 'grisset' who sold him the ruffles, to the reduced chevalier selling *paté's*, to the *fadé* Count de Bissie who read Shakespeare, to the crowd of minor *croquis*—merely touched, but touched with wonderful art."

After this bow to his Victorian predecessor it is rather sad to hear Mr. H. D. Traill express serious doubts even about Sterne's very survival in our literature as a living writer read by living readers, apart from historians "in the way of business." But move on another generation and what do we find? What has the Edwardian age to say about the *Sentimental Journey*?

Well! at the end of *that* epoch, as late as the year of grace 1910, we have *Sterne, a Study*, by Walter Sichel; and, at last, above that grave out of which the body was snatched some hundred and fifty years ago, the first decade of our twentieth century burns a bonfire of incense and homage.

But what was it in Sterne that Walter Sichel, representing the turn of the centuries in a work published only four years before the first world-war, prizes so intensely and praises so enthusiastically? Is it the invention of Walter and Toby Shandy? Is it the invention of Corporal

Trim ? Is it the idea of a particular philosophic attitude to the cosmos entitled Shandyism, as we speak of Pantagruelism or Utopianism, or even shall we say, Existentialism? Is it something, in fact, that gives us, as Goethe does in *Wilhelm Meister*, or as Kwang-Tze did all those centuries before Christ, a new-old way of taking the world?

Not at all ! No, it is for none of these things. Is it Sterne's power of giving himself up, body and soul, to the intoxicating sensation of love, in the way Keats did, till the maddening sorcery of *that girl* soaked with the blood of his lungs as well as with the tears of his passion "the large pillow," which, so he tells his Crazy Castle friend, he had with commendable prescience spread on the floor of his coach for his last journey to Yorkshire ?

Is this subtlest of all Sterne's admirers tempted even for a second to mutter over that fevered pillow as the coach's lamps flicker across the moors:

"She dwells with beauty, beauty that must die,
And joy whose hand is ever at his lips,
Bidding adieu, and aching pleasure nigh,
Turning to poison while the bee-mouth sips" ?

Listen to this comment from this sympathetic critic. "Poor sick-headed, sick-hearted Yorick !" he exclaims, repeating the stricken man's own words, "Eliza has made a shadow of him—and a bore. He breaks another vessel, the blood mingles with his tears, and the doctors assign a cause for his malady which shocks while it amuses him. Yet he retails it all, not only to Eliza, but afterwards in a published letter to Lord Shelburne.

"No detail is too minute (or gross) for him to notice. He is to run through a course of Van Sweeten's corrosive mercury, or rather Van Sweeten's course of corrosive mercury 'is to run through' him. He will be 'sub-limated,' he sighs, to some ethereal substance by the time his Eliza sees him; but he was ever, he adds, 'transparent and a Being easy to See through.'"

One reader at least—nearly forty years after Walter Sichel shuddered at this—can only hope that Lord Shel-burne, as well as the young girl-rebel, had enough human "sentimentality," mixed with enough Aristophanic Attic salt, if not "mercury," to be most shrewdly hit, well! by the tone anyway, in which are revealed these "minute (or gross) details."

The final verdict which Sterne's 1910 admirer pro-nounces upon this "Journal to Eliza," printed at the end of his "study," a journal that has for me the same vibrant and desperate feeling that some have found so painful and even shameful in the letters of Keats to Miss Brawne, is simply to remark that there is "little to relieve these nauseous pages."

Surely when a man is desperately in love, and at the same time is dying of tuberculosis, even if such a man *is* a pro-fessional jester and a married clergyman, something beyond the purely aesthetic attitude in a critic seems legitimate if not absolutely indicated?

There was something however about the special kind of social gaiety, with its "after-us-the-deluge" distractions, and its richly frivolous rather than aristocratic taste, which followed Victoria's death, that lent itself to a certain "macabre" intensity, one aspect of which appears in Henry James's later work. And Walter Sichel catches another aspect of it in what he says about the "Cordelia" episode.

This episode is as illuminating for the understanding of Sterne's complicated "psyche" as anything in his life, and the antipodal difference between it and the scene in

Tristram Shandy where "my Father," overpowered by the bad news about Tristram's nose being hurt in the process of his birth, "threw himself prostrate across his bed" and where, "upon an old set-stich'd chair, valanced and fringed around with party-coloured worsted bobs that stood at the bed's head," my Uncle Toby sat him down, is as perfect an example as could possible be found of the two opposite poles, the homely, musty-fusty, humorous one, and the fantastical dream-woven, hypnerotomachial one, that pivot the circle, so to say, of the compass of his sensitivity.

Cordelia was the imaginary phantom of a mediaeval nun that Sterne's imagination had invented for its sensual, sentimental, and romantic enjoyment. I was on the verge of saying for its *secret* enjoyment; but though no eye could see him dallying with his ghostly Religieuse, this unearthly amour, which lasted a good deal longer than Poe's with his imaginary Ulalume, was the reverse of a "secret" with his more intimate correspondents.

But how strange to think that this cloistered wraith with whose cross suspended between its girlish breasts he imagines himself playing as the two sat together in that rain-swept roofless abbey-ruin a league or two from his parsonage-door was a creation of the same fancy that conjured up those party-coloured worsted bobs of the chair by Mr. Shandy's bed !

If in his last sickness his Loves seemed to float round each other and even to grow confused with one another, so that both the phantom Cordelia and the ocean-wafted Eliza seemed to be invoked—when Lydia re-sorted his letters—in the very cadences he had used for his now brain-sick Lizzie, it was as though Destiny yielding for once to the tantalized longings of our mortal senses had permitted him before he died to drain to their uttermost delicious dregs the tragic-sweet "grapes of Proserpine," and be among "her cloudy trophies hung !"

Afraid of death he never was, nor was he in the habit of sentimentalizing, for all his invention of the word, his own mortal sickness. Exquisitely self-conscious, feverishly sensational, as he was, there was a real stoicism in his powers of endurance; and below his jesting and fooling there was a spirit in him that defied the changes and chances of a not over-lucky clergyman's life.

And this naturally leads us to one of the most mysterious and fascinating of literary problems; namely, how it is that this fantastical "clerk in holy orders" who only plunged into print in the last years of his life when his death from tuberculosis was already visible, was allowed by fate to evoke a couple of characters so striking in their originality as "my Uncle Toby" and Corporal Trim and so enhanced by the presence of "my Father," "my Mother," Doctor Slop and the rest, that they enter by a kind of aesthetic free-masonry the Elysian company of such quintessential inventions as Falstaff and Panurge ? While this in turn slides into that ultimate literary mystery, namely what are the secret aesthetic laws that involve us ourselves, in our rôle as posterity, in the glory or the shame of adding a vital touch to these creations ?

What is the magic in this queer genius of Sterne, light as a feather, airy as gossamer, wayward and unexpected as cuckoo-spit, that it should have lent itself to that strange creative *partnership* between author and posterity referred to by Croce, by means of which we ourselves, anonymous readers of the successive years, have the privilege of adding our quota to that generative power in humanity by which the gods themselves are kept alive, and by which *finis* is never written either on that creaking hinge at Shandy Hall or on the echoing spade in the burying-ground of Elsinore ?

I think the particular quality in the art of Sterne which strikes a devotee most sharply on re-reading the *Sentimental Journey* is his amazing gift for what might be called "Dumb Show" or "Significant Gesturing" or the Tragic-Comic "Language of Signs".

We are constantly being reminded of the Philosophic Debate before that crowded audience in Paris when Panurge argued with Thaumast the Englishman; only the silent gestures in the *Sentimental Journey*, as when Yorick's landlord draws away from him, when he is in trouble about the passport, whereas his valet La Fleur draws nearer, hit us a bit more closely.

"The master of the hotel retired three steps from me, as from an infected person, as I declared this—and poor La Fleur advanced three steps towards me and with that sort of movement which a good soul makes to succour a distressed one—the fellow won my heart by it; and from that single *trait*, I knew his character as perfectly, and could rely upon it as firmly, as if he had served me with fidelity for seven years."

But Sterne himself discusses the whole thing and uses the curious word "translation" to describe its interpretation when at the Opéra Comique the Sentimental traveller enters the Box where an old French officer is reading what might have been the book of the opera. "As soon as I sat down he took his spectacles off and putting them into a shagreen case return'd them and the book into his pocket together. I half rose up and made him a bow."

The most notorious example in the *Sentimental Journey* of the dumb-show pathos of which Sterne is such a master is the dead donkey of Nampont. This is the scene on which Thackeray animadverts in the following tone, a tone that even the judicious Traill feels is "not entirely deserved."

And the amusing thing is that the sneering contemptuous man-of-the-world tone adopted by Thackeray is expressed in the precise kind of familiar, easy, colloquial style which he borrowed, and it is one of the most interesting plagiarisms in our literature, root and branch from Sterne himself: "It is skilfully done that dead jackass . . . Psha ! Mountebank ! I'll not give thee one penny-piece for that trick, donkey and all."

Byron too said the same sort of thing a generation nearer our author's age; but so say *not* I. But come ! Let some youthful Sterne-lover of our present time be the judge in this nice point, for I cannot believe that a generation influenced by Kafka and Camus will cast their vote for Thackeray as against Sterne.

Yes, to an Aristophanic court of our own day let me submit the case. The body of the dead beast does not enter at all; and all its owner does is to sit down on a bench outside his lodging with the ass's bridle and bit carefully placed beside him. Then he takes some bread out of his wallet; and as he has done in a thousand queer places between the borders of Germany and Spain for several years for his living companion he lays a piece of crust "upon the bit of his ass's bridle—looked wistfully at the little arrangement he had made—and then gave a sigh. The simplicity of his grief drew numbers about him——"

But at this point Mr. Traill interrupts against the defendant: "Simplicity indeed of a marvellous sort which could show itself by so extraordinary a piece of acting as this ! . . . Is it true that in *any* country grief—real unaffected, unselfconscious grief—ever did, or ever could display itself by such a trick as that of laying a piece of bread on the bit of a dead ass's bridle ?"

But what neither Thackeray nor Traill are psychologists enough to recognize is that in this confused, tragical-comical and crazy world the impish Pierrot of the Poignant doesn't always obediently submit to the conventional orders of club-room or common-room condemning its appearance as inopportune, improper, and improbable.

"People are so different," as the Colonel said when he caught Lieutenant Jaques after a bloody battle comforting a mewing kitten; and though it might not appeal to us to do what this particular wanderer did there are lots of us childish enough to want to make "our little arrangements" and go through some foolish ritual in regard to the death of a companion even if that companion were many degrees lower, in society's tiresome and ridiculous hierarchy, than an ass.

In the case of Maria of Moulines, though I daresay, if craftily transported from prose to poetry, she would have made a fine subject for a Wordsworthian poem, I confess I feel a little differently. For sex enters here. And where sex enters . . .

At the moment I have three versions in different print before me as I contemplate this scene and one of these, one that Lydia might have given to Eliza, has the picture of Maria on the arm of the Traveller, while in his other hand he holds, so I like to think, the pocket handkerchief marked with an "S" for Shandy.

But it was Yorick's own handkerchief that was now brought into play: "Thou shalt not leave me, Sylvio," said she.

"I look'd in Maria's eyes and saw she was thinking more of her father than of her lover or her little goat; for as she utter'd them"—and a beautiful example is this, by the way, of a great stylist's confidence in his readers' intelligence, for it is we who have to substitute in silence "these words" for this startling "them" though I daresay Mr. Shandy Senior would find a Greek term for such a usage—"as she uttered them, tears trickled down her cheeks.

"I sat close by her and Maria let me wipe them away as they fell with my handkerchief—I then steep'd it in my own—and then in hers—and then in mine—and then I wip'd hers again—and as I did it I felt such undescribable emotions within me as I am sure could not be accounted for from any combinations of matter and motion.

"I am positive I have a soul; nor can all the books with which materialists have pestered the world ever convince me to the contrary."

Nothing could be more revealing of the secret of Sterne's erotic nature than this. He is "positive he has a soul" as we all are, from Socrates to St. Paul, and St. Paul to Dostoievsky, when the Water-spout from the bottom-of-the-sea of sublimated or perverted, or puritanically dam'd up sex-ecstasy bursts heavenward and touches the margin of the next dimension.

But all these tears in Sterne's writings—though we must remember that in the letter he wrote ten days before his death he tells his "unsentimental" friend Mrs. James "To bottle up her tears for him and never draw the cork"— were undoubtedly the expression of an emotion towards the "woman-soul" in life itself, an emotion that though it included his sex-feelings for the women he loved was a curious and quite personal response to life.

Goethe in Faust calls *blood* a very curious "juice"; and the salt water of human tears is another of these curious "juices" that unite us with "the Mothers"; and it may easily turn out that the stress we lay to-day upon our sadist-masochist feelings does not cover as much ground as we imagine. There may be also room for other sorts of tears.

Sterne has been cursed by some for his "indecencies" and they certainly sprinkle his pages as broken shells sprinkle the sands, but no imaginable perversity of human lechery could derive the faintest flicker of real sensual excitement from these folderols of the bawdy and flibbertigibbets of the obscene.

But perhaps this rapturous wiping away of tears from girls' cheeks is no indecency at all, but, like Mephistopheles' lecherous attraction to the angels at the end of Faust, something that can save a soul that is being damned by disarming the very devil that is damning it.

But "people are so different," different sometimes from themselves, and the really powerful and pitiful imagination in Sterne's sensitive nerves has had an influence out of all proportion to the frivolous and flighty manner in which he so often expressed it.

It has had its place, and no mean place either, in influencing the work of those heart-sick servants of pity among us who "rest not by day or by night" in their haunted struggle to save the "lower orders" of animals from those abominable antics of so-called "scientific research" to which it is certain our descendants will look back as we look back to slavery and the inquisition.

But for myself if you were to ask me what are my favourite chapters in the *Sentimental Journey*, though they are not really "chapters", for this man's genius is like a winding river; and they are the pools, the shallows, the rapids, and the curves of a stream of humorous and mischievous invention that never quite reaches the sea and never quite sinks into the earth, I would answer without a second's hesitation: Those two surprising and lovely "vignettes" so closely connected together that begin with Sunday in Paris, and La Fleur bringing our traveller his coffee.

"He had brought the little print of butter upon a currant leaf; and as the morning was warm he had begg'd a sheet of waste paper to put betwixt the currant leaf and his hand. . . .

"When I had finished the butter, I threw the currant leaf out of the window, and was going to do the same by the waste paper—but stopping to read a line first, and that drawing me on to a second and a third—I thought it better worth; so I shut the window and drawing a chair up to it, I sat down to read it.

"It was in the old French of Rabelais' time. . . ." And then there follows the exquisite "vignette" of the Notary, who, "not caring to lie in the same bed with a woman who had but that moment sent him pell-mell to the devil, went forth with his hat and cane and short cloak, the night being very windy, and walk'd out ill at ease towards the Pont Neuf."

Having lost his hat in crossing the bridge he goes down a dark passage and is finally summoned into a large dismantled chamber where an old gentleman requests him to write down what he dictates—"by which", said he, clasping his hands together, "I am to be condemned or acquitted !"—and at this point with one of those perfect touches of minute visualization that are so characteristic of our author—"the Notary held up the point of his pen betwixt the taper and his eye——"

I would indeed recommend any "sensitive" reader of either sex, for *that*, put simply, is all that Sterne's invented word "sentimental" really means, who may at this moment be fingering the leaves of this exquisite book and wondering whether he can afford it, to turn to the "chapter"—only it isn't a chapter—entitled "Le Dimanche, Paris"—and read straight on to the final sentence of the three paragraphs upon flattery entitled the "Riddle Explained."

If, when this is done, a natural human desire to shoot the rapids of "the man Sterne's" eddying and flickering style takes hold upon you, though you still hesitate to put the book in your pocket, flip the pages back a little from where you started and begin again with the end of the passage entitled "the Conquest," meaning of course our traveller's conquest of his lecherous impulse.

"As I finished my address I raised the fair *fille de chambre* up by the hand and led her out of the room—she stood by me till I locked the door and put the key in my pocket—*and then*—the victory being quite decisive—and not till then, I press'd my lips to her cheek, and, taking her by the hand again, led her safe to the gate of the hotel."

This is immediately followed by one of the most beautifully shadowy of all the unpredictable windings of this erratic stream; and by the time you have drifted through the paragraphs entitled "a Mystery" you will, I feel confident, be convinced that it is only by carrying this book about with you until you know its indescribable fits and starts by heart that you will touch the edge of the evasive secret of the most natural, the most careless, and yet the most self-conscious of all our great stylists.

JOHN COWPER POWYS

A SENTIMENTAL JOURNEY
THROUGH FRANCE & ITALY

T HEY order, said I, this matter better in
France——

You have been in France? said my gentleman, turning
quick upon me with the most civil triumph in the world.
Strange! quoth I, debating the matter with myself, that one
and twenty miles sailing, for 'tis absolutely no further from
Dover to Calais, should give a man these rights. I'll look
into them: so giving up the argument I went straight to my
lodgings, put up half a dozen shirts and a black pair of
silk breeches—"the coat I have on," said I, looking at the

sleeve, "will do"—took a place in the Dover stage; and the packet sailing at nine the next morning, by three I had got sat down to my dinner upon a fricasseed chicken, so incontestibly in France, that had I died that night of an indigestion, the whole world could not have suspended the effects of the *Droits d'aubaine*[1]; my shirts, and black pair of silk breeches, portmanteau and all must have gone to the King of France, even the little picture which I have so long worn, and so often have told thee, Eliza, I would carry with me into my grave, would have been torn from my neck. Ungenerous ! to seize upon the wreck of an unwary passenger, whom your subjects had beckon'd to their coast. By heaven ! SIRE, it is not well done; and much does it grieve me, 'tis the monarch of a people so civilized and courteous, and so renowned for sentiment and fine feelings, that I have to reason with.

But I have scarce set foot in your dominions——

---

[1] All the effects of strangers (Swiss and Scotch excepted) dying in France, are seized by virtue of this law, though the heir be upon the spot —the profit of these contingencies being farmed, there is no redress.

CALAIS

When I had finished my dinner, and drank the King of France's health, to satisfy my mind that I bore him no spleen, but, on the contrary, high honour for the humanity of his temper, I rose up an inch taller for the accommodation.

No, said I, the Bourbon is by no means a cruel race: they may be misled like other people; but there is a mildness in their blood. As I acknowledged this, I felt a suffusion of a finer kind upon my cheek—more warm and friendly to man than what Burgundy (at least of two livres a bottle, which was such as I had been drinking) could have produced.

Just God! said I, kicking my portmanteau aside, what is there in this world's goods which should sharpen our spirits, and make so many kind-hearted brethren of us fall out so cruelly as we do by the way?

When man is at peace with man, how much lighter than a feather is the heaviest of metals in his hand! he pulls out his purse, and holding it airily and uncompress'd, looks round him, as if he sought for an object to share it with. In doing this, I felt every vessel in my frame dilate, the arteries beat all chearily together, and every power which sustained life, performed it with so little friction, that 'twould have confounded the most *physical precieuse* in France: with all her materialism, she could scarce have called me a machine.

I'm confident, said I to myself, I should have overset her creed.

The accession of that idea carried Nature, at that time, as high as she could go: I was at peace with the world before, and this finish'd the treaty with myself.

Now, was I a King of France, cried I, what a moment for an orphan to have begg'd his father's portmanteau of me!

THE MONK — CALAIS

I had scarce uttered these words, when a poor monk of the order of St. Francis came into the room to beg something for his convent. No man cares to have his virtues the sport of contingencies, or one man may be generous, as another man is puissant—*sed non quo ad hanc*, or, be it as it may—for there is no regular reasoning upon the ebbs and flows of our humours; they may depend upon the same causes, for aught I know, which influence the tides themselves—'twould oft be no discredit to us to suppose it was so: I'm sure at least for myself, that in many a case I should be more highly satisfied, to have it said by the world, "I had had an affair with the moon, in which there was neither sin nor shame," than have it pass altogether as my own act and deed, wherein there was so much of both.

But be this as it may. The moment I cast my eyes upon him, I was predetermined not to give him a single sous; and accordingly I put my purse into my pocket, button'd it up, set myself a little upon my centre, and advanced up gravely to him: there was something, I fear, forbidding in my look: I have his figure this moment before my eyes, and think there was that in it which deserved better.

The monk, as I judged from the break in his tonsure, a few scatter'd white hairs upon his temples being all that remained of it, might be about seventy, but from his eyes, and that sort of fire which was in them, which seemed more temper'd by courtesy than years, could be no more than sixty. Truth might lie between. He was certainly sixty-five; and the general air of his countenance, notwithstanding something seem'd to have been planting wrinkles in it before their time, agreed to the account.

It was one of those heads which Guido has often painted—mild, pale, penetrating, free from all common-place ideas of fat contented ignorance looking downwards upon the earth: it look'd forwards; but look'd, as if it look'd at something beyond this world. How one of his orders came by it, heaven above, who let it fall upon a monk's shoulders, best knows; but it would have suited a Bramin, and had I met it upon the plains of Indostan, I had reverenced it.

The rest of his outline may be given in a few strokes; one might put it into the hands of any one to design, for 'twas neither elegant or otherwise, but as character and expression made it so: it was a thin, spare form, something above the common size, if it lost not the distinction by a bend forward in the figure—but it was the attitude of Entreaty; and as it now stands presented to my imagination, it gain'd more than it lost by it.

When he had entered the room three paces, he stood still; and laying his left hand upon his breast (a slender white staff with which he journey'd being in his right), when I had got close up to him, he introduced himself with the little story of the wants of his convent, and the poverty of his order, and did it with so simple a grace, and such an air of deprecation was there in the whole cast of his look and figure, I was bewitch'd not to have been struck with it——

A better reason was, I had predetermined not to give him a single sous.

THE MONK — CALAIS

'Tis very true, said I, replying to a cast upwards with his eyes, with which he had concluded his address; 'tis very true—and heaven be their resource who have no other but the charity of the world, the stock of which, I fear, is no way sufficient for the many *great claims* which are hourly made upon it.

As I pronounced the words *great claims*, he gave a slight glance with his eye downwards upon the sleeve of his tunic. I felt the full force of the appeal. I acknowledge it, said I—a coarse habit, and that but once in three years, with meagre diet, are no great matters; and the true point of pity is, as they can be earn'd in the world with so little industry, that your order should wish to procure them by pressing upon a fund which is the property of the lame, the blind, the aged, and the infirm. The captive who lies down counting over and over again the days of his afflictions, languishes also for his share of it; and had you been of the *order of mercy*, instead of the order of St. Francis, poor as I am, continued I, pointing at my portmanteau, full chearfully should it have been open'd to you, for the ransom of the unfortunate. The monk made me a bow. But of all others, resumed I, the unfortunate of our own country, surely, have the first rights; and I have left thousands in distress upon our own shore. The monk gave a cordial wave with his head as much as to say, No doubt, there is misery enough in every corner of the world, as well as within our convent. But we distinguish, said I, laying my hand upon the sleeve of his tunic, in return for his appeal—we distinguish, my good father! betwixt those who wish only to eat the bread of their own labour and those who eat the bread of other people's, and have no other plan in life, but to get through it in sloth and ignorance, *for the love of God*.

The poor Franciscan made no reply: a hectic of a moment pass'd across his cheek, but could not tarry— Nature seemed to have done with her resentments in him; he shewed none—but letting his staff fall within his arm, he press'd both his hands with resignation upon his breast, and retired.

THE MONK — CALAIS

My heart smote me the moment he shut the door. Psha! said I, with an air of carelessness, three several times. But it would not do: every ungracious syllable I had utter'd, crowded back into my imagination: I reflected I had no right over the poor Franciscan, but to deny him; and that the punishment of that was enough to the disappointed, without the addition of unkind language. I considered his grey hairs. His courteous figure seem'd to re-enter and gently ask me what injury he had done me, and why I could use him thus? I would have given twenty livres for an advocate. I have behaved very ill, said I within myself; but I have only just set out upon my travels; and shall learn better manners as I get along.

THE DESOBLIGEANT — CALAIS

When a man is discontented with himself, it has one advantage however, that it puts him into an excellent frame of mind for making a bargain. Now there being no travelling through France and Italy without a chaise, and nature generally prompting us to the thing we are fittest for, I walk'd out into the coach-yard to buy or hire something of that kind to my purpose: an old *Desobligeant*[1] in the furthest corner of the court hit my fancy at first sight, so I instantly got into it; and finding it in tolerable harmony with my feelings, I ordered the waiter to call Monsieur Dessein, the master of the hotel, but Monsieur Dessein being gone to vespers, and not caring to face the Franciscan, whom I saw on the opposite side of the court in conference with a lady just arrived at the inn, I drew the taffeta curtain betwixt us, and being determined to write my journey, I took out my pen and ink, and wrote the preface to it in the *Desobligeant*.

[1] A chaise, so called in France, from its holding but one person.

It must be observed by many a peripatetic philosopher, That nature has set up by her own unquestionable authority certain boundaries and fences to circumscribe the discontent of man: she has effected her purpose in the quietest and easiest manner, by laying him under almost insuperable obligations to work out his ease, and to sustain his suffering at home. It is there only that she has provided him with the most suitable objects to partake of his happiness, and bear a part of that burden, which, in all countries and ages, has ever been too heavy for one pair of shoulders. 'Tis true, we are endued with an imperfect power of spreading our happiness sometimes beyond *her* limits, but 'tis so ordered, that, from the want of languages, connections, and dependencies, and from the difference in educations, customs, and habits, we lie under so many impediments in communicating our sensations out of our own sphere, as often amount to a total impossibility.

It will always follow from hence, that the balance of sentimental commerce is always against the expatriated adventurer: he must buy what he has little occasion for, at their own price; his conversation will seldom be taken in exchange for theirs without a large discount—and this, by the by, eternally driving him into the hands of more equitable brokers for such conversation as he can find, it requires no great spirit of divination to guess at his party——

This brings me to my point; and naturally leads me (if the see-saw of this *Desobligeant* will but let me get on) into the efficient as well as the final causes of travelling——

Your idle people that leave their native country and go abroad for some reason or reasons which may be derived from one of these general causes——

Infirmity of body,
Imbecility of mind, or
Inevitable necessity.

The two first include all those who travel by land or by water, labouring with pride, curiosity, vanity, or spleen, subdivided and combined *in infinitum*.

The third class includes the whole army of peregrine martyrs; more especially those travellers who set out upon their travels with the benefit of the clergy, either as delinquents travelling under the direction of governors recommended by the magistrate—or young gentlemen transported by the cruelty of parents and guardians, and travelling under the direction of governors recommended by Oxford, Aberdeen, and Glasgow.

There is a fourth class, but their number is so small that they would not deserve a distinction, was it not necessary in a work of this nature to observe the greatest precision and nicety, to avoid a confusion of character. And these men I speak of, are such as cross the seas and sojourn in a land of strangers, with a view of saving money for various reasons and upon various pretences: but as they might also save themselves and others a great deal of unnecessary trouble by saving their money at home—and as their reasons for travelling are the least complex of any other species of emigrants, I shall distinguish these gentlemen by the name of

Simple Travellers.

Thus the whole circle of travellers may be reduced to the following *heads*:

       Idle Travellers,
          Inquisitive Travellers,
            Lying Travellers,
               Proud Travellers,
                  Vain Travellers,
                    Splenetic Travellers.

Then follow
    The Travellers of Necessity,
    The delinquent and felonious Traveller,
    The unfortunate and innocent Traveller,
    The simple Traveller.

And last of all (if you please) The Sentimental Traveller (meaning thereby myself), who have travell'd, and of which I am now sitting down to give an account, as much out of *Necessity*, and the *besoin de Voyager*, as any one in the class.

I am well aware, at the same time, as both my travels and observations will be altogether of a different cast from any of my fore-runners; that I might have insisted upon a whole nitch entirely to myself—but I should break in upon the confines of the *Vain* Traveller, in wishing to draw attention towards me, till I have some better grounds for it, than the mere *Novelty of my Vehicle.* It is sufficient for my reader, if he has been a Traveller himself, that with study and reflection hereupon he may be able to determine his own place and rank in the catalogue—it will be one step towards knowing himself, as it is great odds but he retains some tincture and resemblance of what he imbibed or carried out, to the present hour.

The man who first transplanted the grape of Burgundy to the Cape of Good Hope (observe he was a Dutchman) never dreamt of drinking the same wine at the Cape, that the same grape produced upon the French mountains —he was too phlegmatic for that—but undoubtedly he expected to drink some sort of vinous liquor; but whether good, bad, or indifferent, he knew enough of this world to know, that it did not depend upon his choice, but that what is generally called *chance* was to decide his success: however, he hoped for the best: and in these hopes, by an intemperate confidence in the fortitude of his head, and the depth of his discretion, *Mynheer* might possibly overset both in his new vineyard; and by discovering his nakedness, become a laughing-stock to his people.

Even so it fares with the poor Traveller, sailing and posting through the politer kingdoms of the globe, in pursuit of knowledge and improvements.

Knowledge and improvements are to be got by sailing and posting for that purpose; but whether useful knowledge and real improvements, is all a lottery; and even where the adventurer is successful, the acquired stock must be used with caution and sobriety to turn to any profit. But as the chances run prodigiously the other way, both as to the acquisition and application, I am of opinion, That a man would act as wisely if he could prevail upon himself to live contented without foreign knowledge or foreign improvements, especially if he lives in a country that has no absolute want of either—and indeed, much grief of heart has it oft and many a time cost me, when I have observed how many a foul step the inquisitive Traveller has measured to see sights and look into discoveries; all which, as Sancho Panca said to Don Quixote, they might have seen dry-shod at home. It is an age so full of light, that there is scarce a country or corner of Europe whose beams are not crossed and interchanged with others. Knowledge in most of its branches, and in most affairs, is

like music in an Italian street, whereof those may partake
who pay nothing. But there is no nation under heaven
—and God is my record (before whose tribunal I must
one day come and give an account of this work) that I do
not speak it vauntingly—but there is no nation under
heaven abounding with more variety of learning, where the
sciences may be more fitly woo'd, or more surely won, than
here; where art is encouraged, and will so soon rise high;
where Nature (take her altogether) has so little to answer
for, and, to close all, where there is more wit and variety of
character to feed the mind with. Where then, my dear
countrymen, are you going?

We are only looking at this chaise, said they. Your
most obedient servant, said I, skipping out of it, and
pulling off my hat. We were wondering, said one of them,
who, I found, was an *inquisitive Traveller*, what could
occasion its motion. 'Twas the agitation, said I coolly, of
writing a preface. I never heard, said the other, who was a
simple Traveller, of a preface wrote in a *Desobligeant*. It
would have been better, said I, in a *Vis à Vis*.

As an Englishman does not travel to see Englishmen,
I retired to my room.

I perceived that something darken'd the passage more than myself, as I stepp'd along it to my room; it was effectually Mons. Dessein, the master of the hotel, who had just returned from vespers, and, with his hat under his arm, was most complaisantly following me, to put me in mind of my wants. I had wrote myself pretty well out of conceit with the *Desobligeant*; and Mons. Dessein speaking of it, with a shrug, as if it would no way suit me, it immediately struck my fancy that it belong'd to some *innocent Traveller*, who, on his return home, had left it to Mons. Dessein's honour to make the most of. Four months had elapsed since it had finished its career of Europe in the corner of Mons. Dessein's coach-yard; and having sallied out from thence but a vampt-up business at the first, though it had been twice taken to pieces on Mount Sennis, it had not profited much by its adventures—but by none so little as the standing so many months unpitied in the corner of

44

Mons. Dessein's coach-yard. Much indeed was not to be said for it—but something might—and when a few words will rescue misery out of her distress, I hate the man who can be a churl of them.

Now was I the master of this hotel, said I, laying the point of my fore-finger on Mons. Dessein's breast, I would inevitably make a point of getting rid of this unfortunate *Desobligeant*; it stands swinging reproaches at you every time you pass by it.

Mon Dieu! said Mons. Dessein; I have no interest. Except the interest, said I, which men of a certain turn of mind take, Mons. Dessein, in their own sensations: I'm persuaded, to a man who feels for others as well as for himself, every rainy night, disguise it as you will, must cast a damp upon your spirits. You suffer, Mons. Dessein, as much as the machine.

I have always observed, when there is as much *sour* as *sweet* in a compliment, that an Englishman is eternally at a loss within himself, whether to take it or let it alone: a Frenchman never is: Mons. Dessein made me a bow.

C'est bien vrai, said he. But in this case I should only exchange one disquietude for another, and with loss: figure to yourself, my dear Sir, that in giving you a chaise which would fall to pieces before you would go half way to Paris—figure to yourself how much I should suffer, in giving an ill impression of myself to a man of honour, and lying at the mercy, as I must do, *d'un homme d'esprit*.

The dose was made up exactly after my own prescription; so I could not help taking it, and returning Mons. Dessein his bow, without more casuistry, we walk'd together towards his Remise, to take a view of his magazine of chaises.

IN THE STREET—CALAIS

It must needs be a hostile kind of a world, when the buyer (if it be but of a sorry post-chaise) cannot go forth with the seller thereof into the street, to terminate the difference betwixt them, but he instantly falls into the same frame of mind, and views his conventionist with the same sort of eye, as if he was going along with him to Hyde-park corner to fight a duel. For my own part, being but a poor swordsman, and no way a match for Monsieur Dessein, I felt the rotation of all the movements within me, to which the situation is incident. I looked at Monsieur Dessein through and through, eyed him as he walk'd along in profile, then *en face*; thought he look'd like a Jew, then a Turk, disliked his wig, cursed him by my gods, wished him at the devil.

And is all this to be lighted up in the heart for a beggarly account of three or four louis d'ors, which is the most I can be over-reach'd in? Base passion! said I, turning myself about, as a man naturally does upon a sudden reverse of sentiment; base, ungentle passion! thy hand is against every man, and every man's hand against thee. Heaven forbid! said she, raising her hand up to her forehead, for I had turned full in front upon the lady whom I had seen in conference with the monk—she had followed us unperceived. Heaven forbid, indeed! said I, offering her my own. She had a black pair of silk gloves, open only at the thumb and two fore-fingers, so accepted it without reserve, and I led her up to the door of the Remise.

Monsieur Dessein had *diabled* the key above fifty times before he found out he had come with a wrong one in his hand: we were as impatient as himself to have it open'd; and so attentive to the obstacle, that I continued holding her hand almost without knowing it: so that Monsieur Dessein left us together, with her hand in mine, and with our faces turned towards the door of the Remise, and said he would be back in five minutes.

Now a colloquy of five minutes, in such a situation, is worth one of as many ages, with your faces turned towards the street: in the latter case, 'tis drawn from the objects and occurrences without; when your eyes are fixed upon a dead blank you draw purely from yourselves. A silence of a single moment upon Mons. Dessein's leaving us, had been fatal to the situation—she had infallibly turned about—so I begun the conversation instantly.

But what were the temptations (as I write not to apologize for the weaknesses of my heart in this tour, but to give an account of them) shall be described with the same simplicity, with which I felt them.

THE REMISE DOOR — CALAIS

When I told the reader that I did not care to get out of the *Desobligeant*, because I saw the monk in close conference with a lady just arrived at the inn, I told him the whole truth; for I was full as much restrained by the appearance and figure of the lady he was talking to. Suspicion crossed my brain, and said, he was telling her what had passed; something jarred upon it within me. I wished him at his convent.

When the heart flies out before the understanding, it saves the judgment a world of pains. I was certain she was of a better order of beings; however, I thought no more of her, but went on and wrote my preface.

The impression returned upon my encounter with her in the street; a guarded frankness with which she gave me her hand, shewed, I thought, her good education and her good sense; and as I led her on, I felt a pleasurable ductility about her, which spread a calmness over all my spirits.

Good God ! how a man might lead such a creature as this round the world with him !

I had not yet seen her face—'twas not material; for the drawing was instantly set about, and long before we had got to the door of the Remise, *Fancy* had finish'd the whole head, and pleased herself as much with its fitting her goddess, as if she had dived into the TIBER for it. But thou art a seduced, and a seducing slut; and albeit thou cheatest us seven times a day with thy pictures and images, yet with so many charms dost thou do it, and thou deckest out thy pictures in the shapes of so many angels of light, 'tis a shame to break with thee.

When we had got to the door of the Remise, she withdrew her hand from across her forehead, and let me see the original. It was a face of about six and twenty, of a clear transparent brown, simply set off without rouge or powder. It was not critically handsome, but there was that in it, which, in the frame of mind I was in, attached me much more to it—it was interesting. I fancied it wore the characters of a widow'd look, and in that state of its declension, which had passed the two first paroxysms of sorrow, and was quietly beginning to reconcile itself to its loss—but a thousand other distresses might have traced the same lines; I wish'd to know what they had been and was ready to enquire (had the same *bon ton* of conversation permitted, as in the days of Esdras): "*What aileth thee? and why art thou disquieted? and why is thy understanding troubled?*" In a word, I felt benevolence for her; and resolv'd some way or other to throw in my mite of courtesy, if not of service.

Such were my temptations—and in this disposition to give way to them, was I left alone with the lady with her hand in mine, and with our faces both turned closer to the door of the Remise than what was absolutely necessary.

D

THE REMISE DOOR — CALAIS

This certainly, fair lady! said I, raising her hand up a little lightly as I began, must be one of Fortune's whimsical doings: to take two utter strangers by their hands—of different sexes, and perhaps from different corners of the globe, and in one moment place them together in such a cordial situation as Friendship herself could scarce have achieved for them, had she projected it for a month.

And your reflection upon it, shows how much, Monsieur, she has embarrassed you by the adventure.

When the situation is what we would wish, nothing is so ill-timed as to hint at the circumstances which make it so: you thank Fortune, continued she; you had reason—the heart knew it, and was satisfied; and who but an English philosopher would have sent notice of it to the brain to reverse the judgment?

In saying this she disengaged her hand with a look which I thought a sufficient commentary upon the text.

It is a miserable picture which I am going to give of the weakness of my heart, by owning that it suffered a pain, which worthier occasions could not have inflicted. I was mortified with the loss of her hand, and the manner in which I had lost it carried neither oil nor wine to the wound: I never felt the pain of a sheepish inferiority so miserably in my life.

The triumphs of a true feminine heart are short upon these discomfitures. In a very few seconds she laid her hand upon the cuff of my coat, in order to finish her reply; so some way or other, God knows how, I regained my situation.

She had nothing to add.

I forthwith began to model a different conversation for the lady, thinking from the spirit as well as moral of this, that I had been mistaken in her character; but upon turning her face towards me, the spirit which had animated the reply was fled, the muscles relaxed, and I beheld the same unprotected look of distress which first won me to her interest. Melancholy! to see such sprightliness the prey of sorrow, I pitied her from my soul; and though it may seem ridiculous enough to a torpid heart, I could have taken her into my arms, and cherished her, though it was in the open street, without blushing.

The pulsation of the arteries along my fingers pressing

across hers, told her what was passing within me: she looked down. A silence of some moments followed.

I fear, in this interval, I must have made some slight efforts towards a closer compression of her hand, from a subtle sensation I felt in the palm of my own—not as if she was going to withdraw hers but as if she thought about it—and I had infallibly lost it a second time, had not instinct more than reason directed me to the last resource in these dangers—to hold it loosely and in a manner as if I was every moment going to release it, of myself; so she let it continue till Monsieur Dessein returned with the key; and in the mean time I set myself to consider how I should undo the ill impressions which the poor monk's story, in case he had told it her, must have planted in her breast against me.

THE SNUFF-BOX – CALAIS

The good old monk was within six paces of us, as the idea of him crossed my mind; and was advancing towards us a little out of the line, as if uncertain whether he should break in upon us or no. He stopp'd, however, as soon as he came up to us, with a world of frankness: and having a horn snuff-box in his hand, he presented it open to me. You shall taste mine, said I, pulling out my box (which was a small tortoise one) and putting it into his hand. 'Tis most excellent, said the monk. Then do me the favour, I replied, to accept of the box and all, and when you take a pinch out of it, sometimes recollect it was the peace-offering of a man who once used you unkindly, but not from his heart.

The poor monk blush'd as red as scarlet. *Mon Dieu !* said he, pressing his hands together; you never used me unkindly. I should think, said the lady, he is not likely. I blush'd in my turn; but from what movements I leave to the few who feel to analyse. Excuse me, Madame, replied I, I treated him most unkindly, and from no provocations. 'Tis impossible, said the lady. My God ! cried the monk, with a warmth of asseveration which seem'd not to belong to him, the fault was in me, and in the indiscretion of my zeal. The lady opposed it, and I joined with her in maintaining it was impossible, that a spirit so regulated as his, could give offence to any.

I knew not that contention could be rendered so sweet and pleasurable a thing to the nerves as I then felt it We. remained silent without any sensation of that foolish pain which takes place, when in such a circle you look for ten minutes in one another's faces without saying a word. Whilst this lasted, the monk rubb'd his horn box upon the sleeve of his tunic; and as soon as it had acquired a little air of brightness by the friction he made a low bow, and said, 'twas too late to say whether it was the weakness or goodness of our tempers which had involved us in this contest. But be it as it would, he begg'd we might exchange boxes. In saying this, he presented his to me with one hand, as he took mine from me in the other; and having kissed it, with a stream of good-nature in his eyes, he put it into his bosom and took his leave.

I guard this box, as I would the instrumental parts of my religion, to help my mind on to something better: in truth, I seldom go abroad without it: and oft and many a time have I called up by it the courteous spirit of its owner to regulate my own, in the justlings of the world; they had found full employment for his, as I learnt from his story, till about the forty-fifth year of his age, when upon some military services ill requited, and meeting at the same time with a disappointment in the tenderest of passions, he abandoned the sword and the sex together, and took sanctuary, not so much in his convent as in himself.

I feel a damp upon my spirits, as I am going to add, that in my last return through Calais, upon inquiring after Father Lorenzo, I heard he had been dead near three months, and was buried, not in his convent, but, according to his desire, in a little cemetery belonging to it, about two leagues off. I had a strong desire to see where they had laid him—when upon pulling out his little horn box, as I sat by his grave, and plucking up a nettle or two at the head of it, which had no business to grow there, they all struck together so forcibly upon my affections, that I burst into a flood of tears. But I am as weak as a woman; and I beg the world not to smile, but to pity me.

THE REMISE DOOR — CALAIS

I had never quitted the lady's hand all this time; and had held it so long, that it would have been indecent to have let it go, without first pressing it to my lips: the blood and spirits, which had suffered a revulsion from her, crowded back to her, as I did it.

Now the two travellers, who had spoke to me in the coach-yard, happened at that crisis to be passing by, and observing our communications, naturally took it into their heads that we must be *man and wife* at least; so stopping as soon as they came up to the door of the Remise, the one of them, who was the inquisitive Traveller, ask'd us, if we set out for Paris the next morning? I could only answer for myself, I said; and the lady added, she was for Amiens. We dined there yesterday, said the simple Traveller. You go directly through the town, added the other, in your road to Paris. I was going to return a thousand thanks for the intelligence, *that Amiens was in the road to Paris*; but upon pulling out my poor monk's little horn box to take a pinch of snuff, I made them a quiet bow, and wished them a good passage to Dover. They left us alone.

Now where would be the harm, said I to myself, if I was to beg of this distressed lady to accept of half of my chaise? and what mighty mischief could ensue?

Every dirty passion, and bad propensity in my nature, took the alarm, as I stated the proposition. It will oblige you to have a third horse, said AVARICE, which will put twenty livres out of your pocket. You know not what she is, said CAUTION. Or what scrapes the affair may draw you into, whisper'd COWARDICE.

Depend upon it, Yorick! said DISCRETION, 'twill be said you went off with a mistress, and came by assignation to Calais for that purpose.

You can never after, cried HYPOCRISY aloud, shew your face in the world. Or rise, quoth MEANNESS, in the church. Or be any thing in it, said PRIDE, but a lousy prebendary.

But 'tis a civil thing, said I. And as I generally act from the first impulse, and therefore seldom listen to these cabals, which serve no purpose that I know of, but to encompass the heart with adamant, I turn'd instantly about to the lady.

But she had glided off unperceived, as the cause was pleading, and had made ten or a dozen paces down the street, by the time I had made the determination; so I set off after her with a long stride, to make her the proposal with the best address I was master of; but observing she walk'd with her cheek half resting upon the palm of her hand, with the slow, short-measur'd step of thoughtfulness, and with her eyes, as she went step by step, fixed upon the ground, it struck me, she was trying the same cause herself. God help her! said I, she has some mother-in-law, or tartufish aunt, or nonsensical old woman, to consult upon the occasion, as well as myself: so not caring to interrupt the process, and deeming it more gallant to take her at discretion than surprise, I faced about, and took a short turn or two before the door of the Remise, whilst she walk'd musing on one side.

IN THE STREET—CALAIS

Having, on first sight of the lady, settled the affair in my fancy, "that she was of the better order of beings," and then laid it down as a second axiom, as indisputable as the first, that she was a widow, and wore a character of distress, I went no further; I got ground enough for the situation which pleased me, and had she remained close beside my elbow till midnight, I should have held true to my system, and considered her only under that general idea.

She had scarce got twenty paces distant from me, ere something within me called out for a more particular inquiry. It brought on the idea of a further separation. I might possibly never see her more. The heart is for saving what it can; and I wanted the traces through which my wishes might find their way to her, in case I should never rejoin her myself: in a word, I wish'd to know her name, her family's, her condition; and as I knew the place

58

to which she was going, I wanted to know from whence she came: but there was no coming at all this intelligence: a hundred little delicacies stood in the way. I form'd a score different plans—there was no such thing as a man's asking her directly; the thing was impossible.

A little French *debonaire* captain, who came dancing down the street, shewed me it was the easiest thing in the world; for popping in betwixt us, just as the lady was returning back to the door of the Remise, he introduced himself to my acquaintance, and before he had well got announced, begg'd I would do him the honour to present him to the lady. I had not been presented myself, so turning about to her, he did it just as well by asking her, if she had come from Paris? No, she was going that route, she said. *Vous n'êtes pas de Londre?* She was not, she replied. Then Madame must have come through Flanders—*Apparemment vous êtes Flammande?* said the French captain. The lady answered, she was. *Peut-être de Lisle?* added he. She said, she was not of Lisle. Nor Arras? Nor Cambray? Nor Ghent? Nor Brussels? She answered, she was of Brussels.

He had had the honour, he said, to be at the bombardment of it last war—that it was finely situated, *pour cela*—and full of noblesse when the Imperialists were driven out by the French (the lady made a slight curtsy)—so giving her an account of the affair, and of the share he had had in it—he begg'd the honour to know her name—so made his bow.

Et Madame a son Mari? said he, looking back when he had made two steps, and without staying for an answer danced down the street.

Had I served seven years' apprenticeship to good-breeding, I could not have done as much.

THE REMISE—CALAIS

As the little French captain left us, Mons. Dessein
came up with the key of the Remise in his hand, and
forthwith let us into his magazine of chaises.

The first object which caught my eye, as Mons. Dessein
open'd the door of the Remise, was another old tatter'd
Desobligeant, and notwithstanding it was the exact picture
of that which had hit my fancy so much in the coach-yard
but an hour before, the very sight of it stirr'd up a dis-
agreeable sensation within me now; and I thought 'twas a

churlish beast into whose heart the idea could first enter, to construct such a machine; nor had I much more charity for the man who could think of using it.

I observed the lady was as little taken with it as myself: so Mons. Dessein led us on to a couple of chaises which stood abreast, telling us, as he recommended them, that they had been purchased by my Lord A. and B. to go the *grand tour*, but had gone no further than Paris, so were in all respects as good as new. They were too good—so I pass'd on to a third, which stood behind, and forthwith began to chaffer for the price. But 'twill scarce hold two, said I, opening the door and getting in. Have the goodness, Madame, said Mons. Dessein, offering his arm, to step in. The lady hesitated half a second, and stepp'd in; and the waiter that moment beckoning to speak to Mons. Dessein, he shut the door of the chaise upon us, and left us.

THE REMISE DOOR — CALAIS

C'est bien comique, 'tis very droll, said the lady, smiling, from the reflection that this was the second time we had been left together by a parcel of nonsensical contingencies; *c'est bien comique*, said she.

There wants nothing, said I, to make it so, but the comic use which the gallantry of a Frenchman would put it to—to make love the first moment, and an offer of his person the second.

'Tis their *fort*, replied the lady.

It is supposed so at least, and how it has come to pass, continued I, I know not: but they have certainly got the credit of understanding more of love, and making it better than any other nation upon earth; but for my own part, I think them errant bunglers, and in truth the worst set of marksmen that ever tried Cupid's patience.

To think of making love by *sentiments* !

I should as soon think of making a genteel suit of clothes out of remnants: and to do it—pop—at first sight by declaration, is submitting the offer and themselves with it, to be sifted with all their *pours* and *contres*, by an unheated mind.

The lady attended as if she expected I should go on.

Consider then, Madame, continued I, laying my hand upon hers——

That grave people hate Love for the name's sake——

That selfish people hate it for their own——

Hypocrites for heaven's——

And that all of us, both old and young, being ten times worse frighten'd than hurt by the very *report*——

What a want of knowledge in this branch of commerce a man betrays, who ever lets the word come out of his lips, till an hour or two at least after the time that his silence upon it becomes tormenting. A course of small, quiet attentions, not so pointed as to alarm, nor so vague as to be misunderstood, with now and then a look of kindness, and little or nothing said upon it, leaves Nature for your mistress, and she fashions it to her mind.

Then I solemnly declare, said the lady, blushing, you have been making love to me all this while.

THE REMISE—CALAIS

Monsieur Dessein came back to let us out of the chaise, and acquaint the lady Count de L——, her brother, was just arrived at the hotel. Though I had infinite good-will for the lady, I cannot say that I rejoiced in my heart at the event, and could not help telling her so, for it is fatal to a proposal, Madam, said I, that I was going to make to you.

You need not tell me what the proposal was, said she, laying her hand upon both mine, as she interrupted me. A man, my good Sir, has seldom an offer of kindness to make to a woman, but she has a presentiment of it some moments before.

Nature arms her with it, said I, for immediate preservation. But I think, said she, looking in my face, I had no evil to apprehend, and to deal frankly with you, had determined to accept it. If I had—(she stopped a moment) —I believe your good-will would have drawn a story from me, which would have made pity the only dangerous thing in the journey.

In saying this, she suffered me to kiss her hand twice, and with a look of sensibility mixed with a concern, she got out of the chaise and bid adieu.

IN THE STREET—CALAIS

I never finished a twelve-guinea bargain so expeditiously in my life: my time seemed heavy upon the loss of the lady, and knowing every moment of it would be as two, till I put myself into motion, I ordered post-horses directly, and walked towards the hotel.

Lord! said I, hearing the town-clock strike four, and recollecting that I had been little more than a single hour in Calais.

What a large volume of adventures may be grasped within this little span of life, by him who interests his heart in every thing, and who, having eyes to see what time and chance are perpetually holding out to him as he journeyeth on his way, misses nothing he can *fairly* lay his hands on.

If this won't turn out something, another will. No matter: 'tis an essay upon human nature. I get my labour for my pains—'tis enough—the pleasure of the experiment has kept my senses and the best part of my blood awake, and laid the gross to sleep.

I pity the man who can travel from *Dan* to *Beersheba*, and cry, 'Tis all barren. And so it is; and so is all the world to him, who will not cultivate the fruits it offers. I declare, said I, clapping my hands cheerily together, that was I in a desert, I would find out wherewith in it to call forth my affections. If I could not do better, I would fasten them upon some sweet myrtle, or seek some melancholy cypress to connect myself to. I would court their shade, and greet them kindly for their protection; I would cut my name upon them, and swear they were the loveliest trees throughout the desert: if their leaves wither'd, I would teach myself to mourn, and when they rejoiced, I would rejoice along with them.

The learned SMELFUNGUS travelled from Boulogne to Paris, from Paris to Rome, and so on, but he set out with the spleen and jaundice, and every object he pass'd by was discoloured or distorted. He wrote an account of them, but 'twas nothing but the account of his miserable feelings.

I met Smelfungus in the grand portico of the pantheon —he was just coming out of it. *'Tis nothing but a huge cockpit,*[1] said he. I wish you had said nothing worse of the Venus of Medicis, replied I, for in passing through Florence, I had heard he had fallen foul upon the goddess, and used her worse than a common strumpet, without the least provocation in nature.

I popp'd upon Smelfungus again at Turin, in his return home; and a sad tale of sorrowful adventures he had to tell, "wherein he spoke of moving accidents by flood and field, and of the cannibals which each other eat: the Anthropophagi"—he had been flay'd alive, and bedevil'd, and used worse than St. Bartholomew, at every stage he had come at.

I'll tell it, cried Smelfungus, to the world. You had better tell it, said I, to your physician.

Mundungus, with an immense fortune, made the whole tour; going on from Rome to Naples, from Naples to

[1] *Vide* S——'s Travels.

Venice, from Venice to Vienna, to Dresden, to Berlin, without one generous connection or pleasurable anecdote to tell of; but he had travell'd straight on, looking neither to his right hand or his left, lest Love or Pity should seduce him out of his road.

Peace be to them! if it is to be found; but heaven itself, was it possible to get there with such tempers, would want objects to give it. Every gentle spirit would come flying upon the wings of Love to hail their arrival. Nothing would the souls of Smelfungus and Mundungus hear of, but fresh anthems of joy, fresh raptures of love, and fresh congratulations of their common felicity. I heartily pity them: they have brought up no faculties for this work; and was the happiest mansion in heaven to be allotted to Smelfungus and Mundungus, they would be so far from being happy, that the souls of Smelfungus and Mundungus would do penance there to all eternity.

MONTRIUL

I had once lost my portmanteau from behind my chaise, and twice got out in the rain, and one of the times up to the knees in dirt, to help the postillion to tie it on, without being able to find out what was wanting. Nor was it till I got to Montriul, upon the landlord's asking me if I wanted not a servant, that it occurred to me, that that was the very thing.

A servant! That I do most sadly, quoth I. Because, Monsieur, said the landlord, there is a clever young fellow, who would be very proud of the honour to serve an Englishman. But why an English one, more than any other? They are so generous, said the landlord. I'll be shot if this is not a livre out of my pocket, quoth I to myself, this very night. But they have wherewithal to be so, Monsieur, added he. Set down one livre more for that, quoth I. It was but last night, said the landlord, *qu'un my Lord Anglois presentoit un écu à la fille de chambre. Tant pis, pour Mademoiselle Janatone*, said I.

Now Janatone being the landlord's daughter, and the landlord supposing I was young in French, took the liberty to inform me, I should not have said *tant pis* but, *tant mieux. Tant mieux, toujours, Monsieur*, said he, when there is any thing to be got; *tant pis*, when there is nothing. It comes to the same thing, said I. *Pardonnez moi*, said the landlord.

I cannot take a fitter opportunity to observe, once for all, that *tant pis* and *tant mieux* being two of the great hinges in French conversation, a stranger would do well to set himself right in the use of them, before he gets to Paris.

A prompt French Marquis at our ambassador's table demanded of Mr. H——, if he was Mr. H—— the poet? No, said H—— mildly, *Tant pis*, replied the Marquis.

It is H—— the historian, said another. *Tant mieux*, said the Marquis. And Mr. H——, who is a man of an excellent heart, return'd thanks for both.

When the landlord had set me right in this matter, he called in La Fleur, which was the name of the young man he had spoke of, saying only first, That as for his talents, he would presume to say nothing—Monsieur was the best judge what would suit him; but for the fidelity of La Fleur, he would stand responsible in all he was worth.

The landlord deliver'd this in a manner which instantly set my mind to the business I was upon, and La Fleur, who stood waiting without, in that breathless expectation which every son of nature of us have felt in our turns, came in.

MONTRIUL

I am apt to be taken with all kinds of people at first sight; but never more so, than when a poor devil comes to offer his service to so poor a devil as myself; and as I know this weakness, I always suffer my judgment to draw back something on that very account—and this more or less, according to the mood I am in, and the case, and I may add the gender too, of the person I am to govern.

When La Fleur entered the room, after every discount I could make for my soul, the genuine look and air of the fellow determined the matter at once in his favour; so I hired him first and then began to inquire what he could do: But I shall find out his talents, quoth I, as I want them; besides, a Frenchman can do every thing.

Now poor La Fleur could do nothing in the world but beat a drum, and play a march or two upon the fife. I was determined to make his talents do: and can't say my weakness was ever so insulted by my wisdom, as in the attempt.

La Fleur had set out early in life, as gallantly as most Frenchmen do, with *serving* for a few years: at the end of which, having satisfied the sentiment, and found moreover, That the honour of beating a drum was likely to be its own reward, as it open'd no further track of glory to him, he retired *à ses terres*, and lived *comme il plaisoit à Dieu*—that is to say, upon nothing.

And so, quoth *Wisdom*, you have hired a drummer to attend you in this tour of yours through France and Italy! Psha! said I, and do not one half of our gentry go with a humdrum *compagnon du voyage* the same round, and have the piper and the devil and all to pay besides? When man can extricate himself with an *equivoque* in such an unequal match he is not ill off. But you can do something else, La Fleur? said I. *O qu'oui!* he could make spatterdashes, and play a little upon the fiddle. Bravo! said Wisdom. Why, I play a bass myself, said I; we shall do very well. You can shave, and dress a wig a little, La Fleur? He had all the dispositions in the world. It is enough for heaven! said I, interrupting him, and ought to be enough for me. So supper coming in, and having a frisky English spaniel on one side of my chair, and a French valet, with as much hilarity in his countenance as ever nature painted in one, on the other, I was satisfied to my heart's content with my empire; and if monarchs knew what they would be at, they might be satisfied as I was.

MONTRIUL

As La Fleur went the whole tour of France and Italy with me, and will be often upon the stage, I must interest the reader a little further in his behalf, by saying, that I had never less reason to repent of the impulses which generally do determine me, than in regard to this fellow. He was a faithful, affectionate, simple soul as ever trudged after the heels of a philosopher; and notwithstanding his talents of drum-beating and spatterdash-making, which, though very good in themselves, happened to be of no great service to me, yet was I hourly recompensed by the festivity of his temper. It supplied all defects. I had a constant resource in his looks in all difficulties and distresses of my own—I was going to have added, of his too; but La Fleur was out of the reach of every thing; for whether it was hunger or thirst, or cold or nakedness, or watchings, or whatever stripes of ill luck La Fleur met with in our journeyings, there was no index in his physiognomy to point them out by—he was eternally the same. So that if I am a piece of a philosopher, which Satan now and then puts into my head I am, it always mortifies the pride of the conceit, by reflecting how much I owe to the complexional philosophy of this poor fellow, for shaming me into one of a better kind. With all this, La Fleur had a small cast of the coxcomb, but he seemed at first sight to be more a coxcomb of nature than of art; and before I had been three days in Paris with him he seemed to be no coxcomb at all.

The next morning, La Fleur entering upon his employment, I delivered to him the key of my portmanteau, with an inventory of my half a dozen shirts and silk pair of breeches; and bid him fasten all upon the chaise, get the horses put to, and desire the landlord to come in with his bill.

C'est un garçon de bonne fortune, said the landlord, pointing through the window to half a dozen wenches who had got round about La Fleur, and were most kindly

74

taking their leave of him, as the postillion was leading out the horses. La Fleur kissed all their hands round and round again, and thrice he wiped his eyes, and thrice he promised he would bring them all pardons from Rome.

The young fellow, said the landlord, is beloved by all the town, and there is scarce a corner in Montriul where the want of him will not be felt: he has but one misfortune in the world, continued he, "He is always in love." I am heartily glad of it, said I; 'twill save me the trouble every night of putting my breeches under my head. In saying this, I was making not so much La Fleur's eloge, as my own, having been in love, with one princess or another, almost all my life, and I hope I shall go on so till I die, being firmly persuaded, that if ever I do a mean action, it must be in some interval betwixt one passion and another: whilst this interregnum lasts, I always perceive my heart locked up, I can scarce find in it to give Misery a sixpence; and therefore I always get out of it as fast as I can, and the moment I am rekindled, I am all generosity and good-will again; and would do any thing in the world, either for or with any one, if they will but satisfy me there is no sin in it.

But in saying this, sure I am commending the passion, not myself.

A FRAGMENT

The town of Abdera, notwithstanding Democritus
lived there, trying all the powers of irony and laughter
to reclaim it, was the vilest and most profligate town
in all Thrace. What for poisons, conspiracies, and
assassinations, libels, pasquinades, and tumults, there was
no going there by day; 'twas worse by night.

Now, when things were at the worst, it came to pass,
that the Andromeda of Euripides being represented at
Abdera, the whole orchestra was delighted with it: but of
all the passages which delighted them, nothing operated
more upon their imaginations, than the tender strokes of

76

nature which the poet had wrought up in that pathetic speech of Perseus, *O Cupid, prince of God and men*, etc. Every man almost spoke pure iambics the next day, and talk'd of nothing but Perseus his pathetic address. "O Cupid, prince of God and men." In every street of Abdera, in every house, "O Cupid ! Cupid !" in every mouth, like the natural notes of some sweet melody which drops from it whether it will or no, nothing but "Cupid ! Cupid ! prince of God and men." The fire caught, and the whole city, like the heart of one man, open'd itself to Love.

No pharmacopolist could sell one grain of helebore, not a single armourer had a heart to forge one instrument of death. Friendship and Virtue met together, and kiss'd each other in the street, the golden age returned, and hung over the town of Abdera; every Abderite took his oaten pipe, and every Abderitish woman left her purple web, and chastely sat her down and listened to the song.

'Twas only in the power, says the Fragment, of the God whose empire extendeth from heaven to earth, and even to the depths of the sea, to have done this.

MONTRIUL

When all is ready, and every article is disputed and paid for in the inn, unless you are a little sour'd by the adventure, there is always a matter to compound at the door, before you can get into your chaise, and that is with the sons and daughters of poverty, who surround you. Let no man say, "let them go to the devil." 'Tis a cruel journey to send a few miserables, and they have had sufferings enow without it: I always think it better to take a few sous out in my hand; and I would counsel every gentle traveller to do so likewise; he need not be so exact in setting down his motives for giving them —they will be register'd elsewhere.

For my own part, there is no man gives so little as I do; for few, that I know, have so little to give: but as this was the first public act of my charity in France, I took the more notice of it.

A well-a-way ! said I, I have but eight sous in the world, showing them in my hand, and there are eight poor men and eight poor women for 'em.

A poor tatter'd soul, without a shirt on, instantly withdrew his claim, by retiring two steps out of the circle, and making a disqualifying bow on his part. Had the whole parterre cried out, *Place aux dames*, with one voice, it would not have conveyed the sentiment of a deference for the sex with half the effect.

Just Heaven ! for what wise reasons hast thou ordered it, that beggary and urbanity, which are at such variance in other countries, should find a way to be at unity in this ?

I insisted upon presenting him with a single sous, merely for his *politesse*.

A poor little dwarfish, brisk fellow, who stood over against me in the circle, putting something first under his arm, which had once been a hat, took his snuff-box out of his pocket, and generously offer'd a pinch on both sides of him: it was a gift of consequence, and modestly declined. The poor fellow press'd it upon them with a nod of welcomeness. *Prenez en, prenez*, said he, looking another way; so they each took a pinch. Pity thy box should ever want one, said I to myself; so I put a couple of sous into it, taking a small pinch out of his box to enhance their value, as I did it. He felt the weight of the second obligation more than of the first: 'twas doing him an honour, the other was only doing him a charity, and he made me a bow down to the ground for it.

Here ! said I to an old soldier with one hand, who had been campaign'd and worn out to death in the service; here's a couple of sous for thee. *Vive le Roi !* said the old soldier.

I had then but three sous left: so I gave one, simply *pour l'amour de Dieu*, which was the footing on which it was begg'd. The poor woman had a dislocated hip; so it could not be well upon any other notive.

Mon cher et très charitable Monsieur ! There's no opposing this, said I.

My Lord Anglois ! The very sound was worth the money—so I gave *my last sous for it.* But in the eagerness of giving, I had overlooked a *pauvre honteux,* who had no one to ask a sous for him, and who, I believed, would have perished ere he could have ask'd one for himself; he stood by the chaise, a little without the circle, and wiped a tear from a face which I thought had seen better days. Good God ! said I, and I have not one single sous left to give him. But you have a thousand ! cried all the powers of nature, stirring within me. So I gave him—no matter what—I am ashamed to say *how much,* now, and was ashamed to think how little, then: so if the reader can form any conjecture of my disposition, as these two fixed points are given him, he may judge within a livre or two what was the precise sum.

I could afford nothing for the rest, but *Dieu vous benisse. Et le bon Dieu vous benisse encore,* said the old soldier, the dwarf, etc. The *pauvre honteux* could say nothing: he pull'd out a little handkerchief, and wiped his face as he turned away—and I thought he thanked me more than them all.

THE BIDET

Having settled all these little matters, I got into my post-chaise with more ease than ever I got into a post-chaise in my life; and La Fleur having got one large jack-boot on the far side of a little *bidet*,[1] and another on this (for I count nothing of his legs), he canter'd away before me as happy and as perpendicular as a prince.

But what is happiness! what is grandeur in this painted scene of life! A dead ass, before we had got a league, put a sudden stop to La Fleur's career—his bidet would not pass by it. A contention arose betwixt them, and the

[1] Post-horse.

F

poor fellow was kick'd out of jack-boots the very first kick.

La Fleur bore his fall like a French Christian, saying neither more or less upon it, than, Diable ! so presently got up and came to the charge again astride his bidet, beating him up to it as he would have beat his drum.

The bidet flew from one side of the road to the other, then back again, then this way, then that way, and in short every way but by the dead ass. La Fleur insisted upon the thing—and the bidet threw him.

What's the matter, La Fleur, said I, with this bidet of thine ? *Monsieur*, said he, *c'est un cheval le plus opiniâtre du monde*. Nay, if he is a conceited beast, he must go his own way, replied I. So La Fleur got off him, and giving him a good sound lash, the bidet took me at my word, and away he scamper'd back to Montriul. *Peste !* said La Fleur.

It is not *mal-à-propos* to take notice here, that though La Fleur availed himself but of two different terms of exclamation in this encounter, namely, *Diable !* and *Peste !* that there are nevertheless three in the French language; like the positive, comparative, and superlative, one or the other of which serve for every unexpected throw of the dice in life.

Le Diable ! which is the first, and positive degree, is generally used upon ordinary emotions of the mind, where small things only fall out contrary to your expectations, such as, the throwing once doublets, La Fleur's being kick'd off his horse, and so forth; cuckoldom, for the same reason, is always *Le Diable !*

But in cases where the cast has something provoking in it, as in that of the bidet's running away after, and leaving La Fleur aground in jack-boots, 'tis the second degree.

'Tis then *Peste !*

And for the third——

But here my heart is wrung with pity and fellow-feeling, when I reflect what miseries must have been their lot, and how bitterly so refined a people must have smarted, to have forced upon them the use of it.

Grant me, O ye powers which touch the tongue with eloquence in distress !—whatever is my *cast*, grant me but decent words to exclaim in, and I will give my nature way.

But as these were not to be had in France, I resolved to take every evil just as it befel me, without any exclamation at all.

La Fleur, who had made no such covenant with himself, followed the bidet with his eyes till it was got out of sight ; and then, you may imagine, if you please, with what word he closed the whole affair.

As there was no hunting down a frightened horse in jack-boots, there remained no alternative but taking La Fleur either behind the chaise, or into it.

I preferred the latter, and in half an hour we got to the post-house at Nampont.

NAMPONT—THE DEAD ASS

And this, said he, putting the remains of a crust into his wallet, and this should have been thy portion, said he, hadst thou been alive to have shared it with me. I thought by the accent, it had been an apostrophe to his child; but 'twas to his ass, and to the very ass we had seen dead in the road, which had occasioned La Fleur's misadventure. The man seemed to lament it much; and it instantly brought into my mind Sancho's lamentation for his; but he did it with more true touches of nature.

The mourner was sitting upon a stone-bench at the door, with the ass's pannel and its bridle on one side, which he took up from time to time, then laid them down, look'd at them and shook his head. He then took his crust of bread out of his wallet again, as if to eat it; held it some time in his hand, then laid it upon the bit of his ass's bridle, looked wistfully at the little arrangement he had made, and then gave a sigh.

The simplicity of his grief drew numbers about him, and La Fleur amongst the rest, whilst the horses were getting ready; as I continued sitting in the post-chaise, I could see and hear over their heads.

He said he had come from Spain, where he had been from the furthest borders of Franconia; and had got so far on his return home, when his ass died. Every one seemed desirous to know what business could have taken so old and poor a man so far a journey from his own home.

It had pleased Heaven, he said, to bless him with three sons, the finest lads in all Germany; but having in one week lost two of the eldest of them by the small-pox, and the youngest falling ill of the same distemper, he was afraid of being bereft of them all; and made a vow, if Heaven would not take him from him also, he would go in gratitude to St. Iago in Spain.

When the mourner got thus far on his story, he stopp'd to pay nature her tribute and wept bitterly.

He said, Heaven had accepted the conditions, and that he had set out from his cottage with this poor creature, who had been a patient partner of his journey, that it had eat the same bread with him all the way, and was unto him as a friend.

Every body who stood about, heard the poor fellow with concern. La Fleur offered him money. The mourner said, he did not want it—it was not the value of the ass, but the loss of him. The ass, he said, he was assured loved him; and upon this told them a long story of a mischance upon their passage over the Pyrenean mountains, which had separated them from each other three days; during which time the ass had sought him as much as he had sought the ass, and that they had neither scarce eat or drank till they met.

Thou hast one comfort, friend, said I, at least, in the loss of thy poor beast; I'm sure thou has been a merciful master to him. Alas! said the mourner, I thought so, when he was alive, but now that he is dead I think otherwise. I fear the weight of myself and my afflictions together have been too much for him—they have shortened the poor creature's days and I fear I have them to answer for. Shame on the world! said I to myself; did we love each other, as this poor soul but loved his ass, 'twould be something.

NAMPONT—THE POSTILLION

The concern which the poor fellow's story threw me into required some attention: the postillion paid not the least to it, but set off upon the *pavé* in a full gallop.

The thirstiest soul in the most sandy desert of Arabia could not have wished more for a cup of cold water, than mine did for grave and quiet movements; and I should have had an high opinion of the postillion, had he but stolen off with me in something like a pensive pace. On the contrary, as the mourner finished his lamentation, the fellow gave an unfeeling lash to each of his beasts, and set off clattering like a thousand devils.

I called to him as loud as I could, for heaven's sake to go slower, and the louder I called, the more unmercifully he galloped. The deuce take him and his galloping too, said I, he'll go on tearing my nerves to pieces till he has worked me into a foolish passion, and then he'll go slow, that I may enjoy the sweets of it.

The postillion managed the point to a miracle: by the time he had got to the foot of a steep hill about half a league from Nampont, he had put me out of temper with him and then with myself, for being so.

My case then required a different treatment; and a good rattling gallop would have been of real service to me.

Then, prithee, get on; get on, my good lad, said I.

The postillion pointed to the hill. I then tried to return back to the story of the poor German and his ass, but I had broke the clue and could no more get into it again, than the postillion could into a trot.

The deuce go, said I, with it all! Here am I sitting as candidly disposed to make the best of the worst, as ever wight was, and all runs counter.

There is one sweet lenitive at least for evils, which Nature holds out to us: so I took it kindly at her hands, and fell asleep; and the first word which roused me was *Amiens*.

Bless me! said I, rubbing my eyes; this is the very town where my poor lady is to come.

AMIENS

The words were scarce out of my mouth when the Count de L——'s post-chaise, with his sister in it, drove hastily by: she had just time to make me a bow of recognition—and of that particular kind of it, which told me she had not yet done with me. She was as good as her look; for, before I had quite finished my supper, her brother's servant came into the room with a billet, in which she said she had taken the liberty to charge me with a letter, which I was to present myself to Madame R—— the first morning I had nothing to do at Paris. There was only added, she was sorry, but from what *penchant* she had not considered, that she had been prevented telling me her story, that she still owed it me; and if my route should ever lay through Brussels, and I had not by then forgot the name of Madame de L——, that Madame de L—— would be glad to discharge her obligation.

Then I will meet thee, said I, fair spirit, at Brussels— 'tis only returning from Italy through Germany to Holland, by the route of Flanders, home—'twill scarce be ten posts out of my way; but were it ten thousand ! with what a moral delight will it crown my journey, in sharing in the sickening incidents of a tale of misery told to me by such a sufferer ! to see her weep ! and though I cannot dry up the fountain of her tears, what an exquisite sensation is there still left, in wiping them away from off the cheeks of the first and fairest of women, as I'm sitting with my handkerchief in my hand in silence the whole night beside her.

There was nothing wrong in the sentiment; and yet I instantly reproached my heart with it in the bitterest and most reprobate of expressions.

It had ever, as I told the reader, been one of the singular blessings of my life, to be almost every hour of it miserably in love with some one; and my last flame happening to be blown out by a whiff of jealousy on the sudden turn of a corner, I had lighted it up afresh at the pure taper of Eliza, but about three months before, swearing as I did it, that it should last me through the whole journey. Why should I dissemble the matter ? I had sworn to her eternal fidelity; she has a right to my whole heart; to divide my affections was to lessen them; to expose them, was to risk them: where there is risk, there may be loss:—and what wilt thou have, Yorick! to answer to a heart so full of trust and confidence, so good, so gentle and unreproaching ?

I will not go to Brussels, replied I, interrupting myself

—but my imagination went on. I recalled her looks at that crisis of our separation, when neither of us had power to say adieu ! I look'd at the picture she had tied in a black ribband about my neck and blush'd as I look'd at it. I would have given the world to have kiss'd it, but was ashamed. And shall this tender flower, said I, pressing it between my hands, shall it be smitten to its very root, and smitten, Yorick ! by thee, who has promised to shelter it in thy breast ?

Eternal fountain of happiness ! said I, kneeling down upon the ground, be thou my witness, and every pure spirit which tastes it, be my witness also, That I would not travel to Brussels, unless Eliza went along with me, did the road lead me towards heaven.

In transports of this kind, the heart, in spite of the understanding, will always say too much.

THE LETTER—AMIENS

Fortune had not smiled upon La Fleur; for he had been unsuccessful in his feats of chivalry, and not one thing had offered to signalize his zeal for my service from the time he had entered into it, which was almost four-and-twenty hours. The poor soul burn'd with impatience; and the Count de L——'s servant coming with the letter, being the first practicable occasion which offered, La Fleur had laid hold of it; and in order to do honour to his master, had taken him into a back parlour in the Auberge, and treated him with a cup or two of the best wine in Picardy; and the Count de L——'s servant, in return, and not to be behind-hand in politeness with La Fleur, had taken him back with him to the Count's hotel. La Fleur's *prevenancy* (for there was a passport in his very looks) soon set every servant in the kitchen at ease with him; and as a Frenchman, whatever be his talents, has no sort of prudery in showing them, La Fleur, in less than five minutes, had pulled out his fife, and leading off the dance himself with the first note, set the *fille de chambre*, the *maitre d'hôtel*, the cook, the scullion, and all the household, dogs and cats, besides an old monkey, a-dancing: I suppose there never was a merrier kitchen since the flood.

Madame de L——, in passing from her brother's apartments to her own, hearing so much jollity below stairs, rung up her *fille de chambre* to ask about it; and hearing it was the English gentleman's servant who had set the whole house merry with his pipe, she ordered him up.

As the poor fellow could not present himself empty, he had loaden'd himself in going up stairs with a thousand compliments to Madame de L——, on the part of his master; added a long apocrypha of inquiries after Madame de L——'s health; told her, that Monsieur his master was *au désespoir* for her re-establishment from the fatigues of her journey; and, to close all, that Monsieur had received the letter which Madame had done him the honour—And he has done me the honour, said Madame de L——, interrupting La Fleur, to send a billet in return.

Madame de L—— had said this with such a tone of reliance upon the fact, that La Fleur had not power to disappoint her expectations. He trembled for my honour, and possibly might not altogether be unconcerned for his own, as a man capable of being attached to a master who could be wanting *en egards vis à vis d'une femme!* so that when Madame de L—— asked La Fleur if he had brought a letter—*O qu'oui*, said La Fleur; so laying down his hat upon the ground, and taking hold of the flap of his right side pocket with his left hand, he began to search for the letter with his right, then contrary-wise. *Diable!* Then sought every pocket, pocket by pocket, round, not forgetting his fob. *Peste!* Then La Fleur emptied them upon the floor; pulled out a dirty cravat, a handkerchief, a comb, a whip-lash, a night-cap, then gave a peep into his hat. *Quelle etourderie !* He had left the letter upon the table in the Auberge—he would run for it, and be back with it in three minutes.

I had just finished my supper when La Fleur came in to give me an account of his adventure: he told the whole story simply as it was; and only added, that if Monsieur had forgot (*par hazard*) to answer Madame's letter, the arrangement gave him an opportunity to recover the *faux pas*—and if not, that things were only as they were.

Now I was not altogether sure of my *etiquette*, whether I ought to have wrote or no; but if I had, a devil himself could not have been angry: 'Twas but the officious zeal of a well-meaning creature for my honour; and however he might have mistook the road, or embarrassed me in so doing, his heart was in no fault, I was under no necessity to write, and what weighed more than all, he did not look as if he had done amiss.

'Tis all very well, La Fleur, said I. 'Twas sufficient. La Fleur flew out of the room like lightning, and return'd with pen, ink, and paper, in his hand; and coming up to the table, laid them close before me, with such a delight in his countenance, that I could not help taking up the pen.

I begun and begun again; and though I had nothing to say, and that nothing might have been expressed in half a dozen lines, I made half a dozen different beginnings, and could no way please myself.

In short, I was in no mood to write.

La Fleur stepp'd out and brought a little water in a glass to dilute my ink, then fetched sand and seal-wax. It was all one; I wrote, and blotted, and tore off, and burnt, and wrote again. *Le diable l'emporte!* said I half to myself; I cannot write this self-same letter; throwing the pen down despairingly as I said it.

As soon as I had cast down the pen, La Fleur advanced with the most respectful carriage up to the table, and making a thousand apologies for the liberty he was going to take, told me he had a letter in his pocket wrote by a drummer in his regiment to a corporal's wife, which, he durst say, would suit the occasion.

I had a mind to let the poor fellow have his humour. Then prithee, said I, let me see it.

La Fleur instantly pulled out a little dirty pocket book cramm'd full of small letters and billet-doux in a sad condition, and laying it upon the table, and then untying the string which held them all together, run them over one by one, till he came to the letter in question. *La voila*, said he, clapping his hands: so unfolding it first, he laid it before me, and retired three steps from the table whilst I read it.

THE LETTER

Madame,

Je suis penetré de la douleur la plus vive, et reduit en même temps au désespoir par ce retour imprevû du Corporal qui rend notre entrevue de ce soir la chose du monde la plus impossible.

Mais vive la joie! et toute la mienne sera de penser à vous.

L'amour n'est _rien_ sans sentiment.

Et le sentiment est encore _moins_ sans amour.

On dit qu'on ne doit jamais se désespérer.

On dit aussi que Monsieur le Corporal monte la garde Mercredi: alors ce sera mon tour.

Chacun à son tour.

En attendant — Vive l'amour! et vive la bagatelle!

Je suis, Madame,

Avec toutes les sentiments les
plus respectueux et les plus
tendres, tout à vous,
Jaques Roque

It was but changing the Corporal into the Count and saying nothing about mounting guard on Wednesday, and the letter was neither right or wrong. So to gratify the poor fellow, who stood trembling, for my honour, his own, and the honour of his letter, I took the cream gently off it, and whipping it up my own way, I seal'd it up and sent him with it to Madame de L——, and the next morning we pursued our journey to Paris.

PARIS

When a man can contest the point by dint of equipage, and carry on all floundering before him with half a dozen lackies and a couple of cooks, 'tis very well in such a place as Paris—he may drive in at which end of a street he will.

A poor prince who is weak in cavalry, and whose whole infantry does not exceed a single man, had best quit the field; and signalize himself in the cabinet, if he can get up into it—I say *up into it*, for there is no descending perpendicular amongst 'em with a "*Me voici, mes enfans*" (here I am), whatever many may think.

I own my first sensations, as soon as I was left solitary and alone in my own chamber in the hotel, were far from being so flattering as I had prefigured them. I walked up gravely to the window in my dusty black coat, and looking through the glass saw all the world in yellow, blue, and green, running at the ring of pleasure. The old with broken lances, and in helmets which had lost their vizards, the young in armour bright which shone like gold, beplumed with each gay feather of the east, all—all—tilting at it like fascinated knights in tournaments of yore for fame and love.

Alas, poor Yorick! cried I, what art thou doing here? On the very first onset of all this glittering clatter thou art reduced to an atom. Seek—seek some winding alley, with a tourniquet at the end of it, where chariot never rolled or flambeau shot its rays: there thou mayest solace thy soul in converse sweet with some kind *grisset* of a barber's wife, and get into such coteries!

May I perish! if I do, said I, pulling out the letter which I had to present to Madame de R——. I'll wait upon this lady the very first thing I do. So I called La Fleur to go seek me a barber directly, and come back and brush my coat.

THE WIG~PARIS

When the barber came, he absolutely refused to have any thing to do with my wig: 'twas either above or below his art: I had nothing to do, but to take one ready made of his own recommendation.

But I fear, friend ! said I, this buckle won't stand. You may immerge it, replied he, into the ocean, and it will stand.

What a great scale is every thing upon in this city ! thought I. The utmost stretch of an English periwig-maker's ideas could have gone no further than to have "dipped it into a pail of water." What difference ! 'tis like time to eternity.

I confess I do hate all cold conceptions, as I do the puny ideas which engender them; and am generally so struck with the great works of nature, that for my own part, if I could help it, I never would make a comparison less than a mountain at least. All that can be said against the French sublime in this instance of it, is this: that the grandeur is *more* in the *word*; and *less* in the *thing*. No doubt the ocean fills the mind with vast ideas; but Paris being so far inland, it was not likely I should run post a hundred miles out of it, to try the experiment—the Parisian barber meant nothing.

The pail of water standing beside the great deep, makes certainly but a sorry figure in speech, but 'twill be said it has one advantage: 'tis in the next room, and the truth of the buckle may be tried in it, without more ado, in a single moment.

In honest truth, and upon a more candid revision of the matter, *The French expression professes more than it performs.*

I think I can see the precise and distinguishing marks of national characters more in these nonsensical *minutuæ*, than in the most important matters of state; where great men of all nations stalk and talk so much alike, that I would not give ninepence to chuse amongst them.

I was so long in getting from under my barber's hands, that it was too late to think of going with my letter to Madame R——that night: but when a man is once dressed at all points for going out, his reflections turn to little account; so taking down the name of the Hôtel de Modene, where I lodged, I walked forth without any determination where to go. I shall consider of that, said I, as I walk along.

Hail ye small sweet courtesies of life, for smooth do ye make the road of it ! like grace and beauty which beget inclinations to love at first sight: 'tis ye who open this door and let the stranger in.

Pray, Madame, said I, have the goodness to tell me which way I must turn to go to the Opera comique. Most willingly, Monsieur, said she, laying aside her work.

I had given a cast with my eye into half a dozen shops as I came along in search of a face not likely to be disordered by such an interruption; till at last, this hitting my fancy, I had walked in.

She was working a pair of ruffles as she sat in a low chair on the far side of the shop facing the door.

Très volontiers ; most willingly, said she, laying her work down upon a chair next her, and rising up from the low chair she was sitting in, with so cheerful a movement and so cheerful a look, that had I been laying out fifty louis d'ors with her, I should have said "This woman is grateful."

You must turn, Monsieur, said she, going with me to the door of the shop, and pointing the way down the street I was to take, you must first turn to your left hand— *mais prenez garde,* there are two turns, and be so good as to take the second—then go down a little way and you'll see a church, and when you are past it, give yourself the trouble to turn directly to the right, and that will lead you to the foot of the *Pont Neuf,* which you must cross; and there any one will do himself the pleasure to shew you.

She repeated her instructions three times over to me, with the same good-natur'd patience the third time as the first; and if *tones and manners* have a meaning, which certainly they have, unless to hearts which shut them out, she seemed really interested, that I should not lose myself.

I will not suppose it was the woman's beauty, notwithstanding she was the handsomest grisset, I think, I ever saw, which had much to do with the sense I had of her courtesy; only I remember, when I told her how much I was obliged to her, that I looked very full in her eyes and that I repeated my thanks as often as she had done her instructions.

I had not got ten paces from the door, before I found I had forgot every tittle of what she had said; so looking back, and seeing her still standing in the door of the shop as if to look whether I went right or not, I returned back, to ask her whether the first turn was to my right or left, for that I had absolutely forgot. Is it possible? said she, half laughing. 'Tis very possible, replied I, when a man is thinking more of a woman than of her good advice.

As this was the real truth she took it, as every woman takes a matter of right, with a slight courtesy.

Attendez, said she, laying her hand upon my arm to detain me, whilst she called a lad out of the back-shop to get ready a parcel of gloves. I am just going to send him, said she, with a packet into that quarter, and if you will have the complaisance to step in, it will be ready in a moment, and he shall attend you to the place. So I walk'd in with her to the far side of the shop, and taking up the ruffle in my hand, which she laid upon the chair, as if I had a mind to sit, she sat down herself in her low chair, and I instantly sat myself down beside her.

He will be ready, Monsieur, said she, in a moment. And in that moment, replied I, most willingly would I say something very civil to you for all these courtesies. Any one may do a casual act of good-nature, but a continuation of them shows it is a part of the temperature; and certainly, added I, if it is the same blood which comes from the heart, which descends to the extremes (touching her wrist), I am sure you must have one of the best pulses of any woman in the world. Feel it, said she, holding out her arm. So laying down my hat, I took hold of her fingers in one hand, and applied the two fore-fingers of my other to the artery.

Would to heaven! my dear Eugenius, thou hadst passed by, and beheld me sitting in my black coat, and in my lack-a-day-sical manner, counting the throbs of it, one by one, with as much true devotion as if I had been watching the critical ebb or flow of her fever! How wouldst thou have laugh'd and moralized upon my new profession ! And thou shouldst have laugh'd and moralized on. Trust me, my dear Eugenius, I should have said, "there are worse occupations in this world *than feeling a woman's pulse*." But a Grisset's ! thou wouldst have said, and in an open shop ! Yorick——

So much the better: for when my views are direct, Eugenius, I care not if all the world saw me feel it.

THE HUSBAND — PARIS

I had counted twenty pulsations, and was going on fast towards the fortieth, when her husband coming unexpected from a back parlour into the shop, put me a little out in my reckoning. 'Twas nobody but her husband, she said, so I began a fresh score. Monsieur is so good, quoth she, as he pass'd by us, as to give himself the trouble of feeling my pulse. The husband took off his hat, and making me a bow, said, I did him too much honour; and having said that, he put on his hat and walk'd out.

Good God! said I to myself, as he went out, and can this man be the husband of this woman?

Let it not torment the few who know what must have been the grounds of this exclamation, if I explain it to those who do not.

In London a shopkeeper and a shopkeeper's wife seem to be one bone and one flesh: in the several endowments of mind and body, sometimes the one, sometimes the other has it, so as in general to be upon a par, and to tally with each other as nearly as a man and wife need to do.

In Paris, there are scarce two orders of beings more different: for the legislative and executive powers of the shop not resting in the husband, he seldom comes there. In some dark and dismal room behind, he sits commerce-less in his thrum night-cap, the same rough son of Nature that Nature left him.

The genius of a people where nothing but the monarchy is *salique*, having ceded this department, with sundry others, totally to the women—by a continual higgling with customers of all ranks and sizes from morning to night, like so many rough pebbles shook long together in a bag, by amicable collisions, they have worn down their asperities and sharp angles, and not only become round and smooth, but will receive, some of them, a polish like a brilliant—Monsieur *le Mari* is little better than the stone under your foot.

Surely, surely, man ! it is not good for thee to sit alone —thou wast made for social intercourse and gentle greet-ings, and this improvement of our natures from it, I appeal to, as my evidence.

And how, how does it beat, Monsieur ? said she. With all the benignity, said I, looking quietly in her eyes, that I expected. She was going to say something civil in return, but the lad came into the shop with the gloves. *A propos*, said I, I want a couple of pair myself.

The beautiful Grisset rose up when I said this, and going behind the counter, reach'd down a parcel and untied it: I advanced to the side over against her: they were all too large. The beautiful Grisset measured them one by one across my hand—it would not alter the dimensions. She begg'd I would try a single pair, which seemed to be the least. She held it open; my hand slipped into it at once. It will not do, said I, shaking my head a little. No, said she, doing the same thing.

There are certain combined looks of simple subtlety, where whim, and sense, and seriousness, and nonsense, are so blended, that all the languages of Babel set loose together could not express them: they are communicated and caught so instantaneously, that you can scarce say which party is the infecter. I leave it to your men of words to swell pages about it—it is enough in the present to say again, the gloves would not do; so folding our hands within our arms, we both loll'd upon the counter. It was narrow, and there was just room for the parcel to lay between us.

The beautiful Grisset look'd sometimes at the gloves, then sideways to the window, then at the gloves, and then at me. I was not disposed to break silence—I follow'd her example: so I look'd at the gloves, then to the window, then at the gloves, and then at her, and so on alternately.

I found I lost considerably in every attack. She had a quick black eye, and shot through two such long and silken eye-lashes with such penetration, that she look'd into my very heart and reins. It may seem strange, but I could actually feel she did.

It is no matter, said I, taking up a couple of the pairs next me, and putting them into my pocket.

I was sensible the beautiful Grisset had not ask'd above a single livre above the price—I wish'd she had ask'd a livre more, and was puzzling my brains how to bring the matter about. Do you think, my dear Sir, said she, mistaking my embarrassment, that I could ask a *sous* too much of a stranger, and of a stranger whose politeness, more than his want of gloves, has done me the honour to lay himself at my mercy? *M'en croyez capable?* Faith! not I, said I; and if you were, you are welcome. So counting the money into her hand, and with a lower bow than one generally makes to a shopkeeper's wife, I went out, and her lad with his parcel followed me.

There was nobody in the box I was let into but a kindly old French officer. I love the character, not only because I honour the man whose manners are softened by a profession which makes bad men worse; but that I once knew one—for he is no more—and why should I not rescue one page from violation by writing his name in it, and telling the world it was Captain Tobias Shandy, the dearest of my flock and friends, whose philanthropy I never think of at this long distance from his death but my eyes gush out with tears. For his sake, I have a predilection for the whole corps of veterans; and so I strode over the two back rows of benches, and placed myself beside him.

The old officer was reading attentively a small pamphlet, it might be the book of the opera, with a large pair of spectacles. As soon as I sat down, he took his spectacles off, and putting them into a shagreen case, return'd them and the book into his pocket together. I half rose up, and made him a bow.

Translate this into any civilised language in the world, the sense is this:

"Here's a poor stranger come into the box—he seems as if he knew nobody and is never likely, was he to be seven years in Paris, if every man he comes near keeps his spectacles upon his nose. 'Tis shutting the door of conversation absolutely in his face, and using him worse than a German."

The French officer might as well have said it all aloud: and if he had, I should in course have put the bow I made him into French too, and told him, "I was sensible of his attention, and return'd him a thousand thanks for it."

There is not a secret so aiding to the progress of sociality, as to get master of this *short hand*, and be quick in rendering the several turns of looks and limbs, with all their inflections and delineations, into plain words. For my own part, by long habitude, I do it so mechanically, that when I walk the streets of London, I go translating all the way; and have more than once stood behind in the circle, where not three words have been said, and have brought off twenty different dialogues with me, which I could have fairly wrote down and sworn to.

I was going one evening to Martini's concert at Milan, and was just entering the door of the hall, when the Marquesina de F—— was coming out in a sort of a hurry, she was almost upon me before I saw her; so I gave a spring to one side to let her pass. She had done the same, and on the same side too: so we ran our heads together: she instantly got to the other side to get out: I was just as unfortunate as she had been; for I had sprung to that side, and opposed her passage again. We both flew together to the other side, and then back, and so on. It was ridiculous.

We both blush'd intolerably. So I did at last the thing I should have done at first: I stood stock still, and the Marquesina had no more difficulty. I had no power to go into her room, till I had made her so much reparation as to wait and follow her with my eye to the end of the passage. She look'd back twice, and walk'd along it rather sideways, as if she would make room for any one coming up stairs to pass her. No, said I; that's a vile translation: the Marquesina has a right to the best apology I can make her; and that opening is left for me to do it in. So I ran and begg'd pardon for the embarrassment I had given her, saying it was my intention to have made her way. She answered, she was guided by the same intention towards me; so we reciprocally thank'd each other. She was at the top of the stairs; and seeing no *chichesbee* near her, I begg'd to hand her to her coach; so we went down the stairs, stopping at every third step to talk of the concert and the adventure. Upon my word, Madame, said I, when I had handed her in, I made six different efforts to let you go out. And I made six efforts, replied she, to let you enter. I wish to heaven you would make a seventh, said I. With all my heart, said she, making room. Life is too short to be long about the forms of it, so I instantly stepp'd in, and she carried me home with her. And what became of the concert, St. Cecilia, who, I suppose, was at it, knows more than I.

I will only add, that the connection which arose out of the translation, gave me more pleasure than any one I had the honour to make in Italy.

THE DWARF—PARIS

I had never heard the remark made by any one in my life, except by one; and who that was will probably come out in this chapter; so that being pretty much unprepossessed, there must have been grounds for what struck me the moment I cast my eyes over the parterre —and that was, the unaccountable sport of nature in forming such numbers of dwarfs. No doubt, she sports at certain times in almost every corner of the world; but in Paris, there is no end to her amusements: the goddess seems almost as merry as she is wise.

As I carried my idea out of the Opera comique with me, I measured every body I saw walking in the streets by it. Melancholy application! especially where the size was extremely little, the face extremely dark, the eyes quick, the nose long, the teeth white, the jaw prominent, to see so many miserables, by force of accidents driven out of their own proper class into the very verge of another, which it gives me pain to write down. Every third man a pigmy!—some by rickety heads and hump backs; others by bandy legs; a third set arrested by the hand of Nature in the sixth and seventh years of their growth; a fourth, in their perfect and natural state like dwarf apple-trees; from the first rudiments and stamina of their existence, never meant to grow higher.

A medical traveller might say, 'tis owing to undue bandages; a splenetic one, to want of air; and an inquisitive traveller, to fortify the system, may measure the height of their houses, the narrowness of their streets, and in how few feet square in the sixth and seventh stories such numbers of the *Bourgeoisie* eat and sleep together; but I remember, Mr. Shandy the elder, who accounted for nothing like any body else, in speaking one evening of these matters, averred, that children, like other animals, might be increased almost to any size, provided they came right into the world; but the misery was, the citizens of Paris were so coop'd up, that they had not actually room enough to get them. I did not call it getting any thing, said he; 'tis getting nothing. Nay, continued he, rising in his argument, 'tis getting worse than nothing, when all you have got, after twenty or five-and-twenty years of the tenderest care and most nutritious aliment bestowed upon it, shall not at last be as high as my leg. Now, Mr. Shandy being very short, there could be nothing more said of it.

As this is not a work of reasoning, I leave the solution as I found it, and content myself with the truth only of the remark, which is verified in every lane and by-lane of Paris. I was walking down that which leads from the Carousal to the Palais Royal, and observing a little boy in some distress at the side of the gutter, which ran down the middle of it, I took hold of his hand, and help'd him over. Upon turning up his face to look at him after, I perceived he was about forty. Never mind, said I;

some good body will do as much for me when I am ninety.

I feel some little principles within me, which incline me to be merciful towards this poor blighted part of my species, who have neither size or strength to get on in the world. I cannot bear to see one of them trod upon; and had scarce got seated beside my old French officer, ere the disgust was exercised, by seeing the very thing happen under the box we sat in.

At the end of the orchestra, and betwixt that and the first side-box, there is a small esplanade left, where, when the house is full, numbers of all ranks take sanctuary. Though you stand, as in the parterre, you pay the same price as in the orchestra. A poor defenceless being of this order had got thrust, somehow or other, into this luckless place; the night was hot, and he was surrounded by beings two feet and a half higher than himself. The dwarf suffered inexpressibly on all sides; but the thing which incommoded him most, was a tall corpulent German, near seven feet high, who stood directly betwixt him and all possibility of his seeing either the stage or the actors. The poor dwarf did all he could to get a peep at what was going forwards by seeking for some little opening betwixt the German's arm and his body, trying first one side, then the other; but as the German stood square in the most unaccommodating posture that can be imagined, the dwarf might as well have been placed at the bottom of the deepest draw-well in Paris; so he civilly reach'd up his hand to the German's sleeve, and told him his distress. The German turn'd his head back, look'd down upon him as Goliath did upon David, and unfeelingly resumed his posture.

I was just then taking a pinch of snuff out of my monk's little horn box. And how would thy meek and courteous

spirit, my dear monk ! so temper'd to *bear and forbear* !
how sweetly would it have lent an ear to this poor soul's
complaint !

The old French officer, seeing me lift up my eyes with
an emotion, as I made the apostrophe, took the liberty to
ask me what was the matter. I told him the story in three
words, and added, how inhuman it was.

By this time the dwarf was driven to extremes, and in
his first transports, which are generally unreasonable, had
told the German he would cut off his long queue with
his knife. The German look'd back coolly, and told him
he was welcome, if he could reach it.

An injury sharpen'd by an insult, be it to whom it will,
makes every man of sentiment a party: I could have
leap'd out of the box to have redressed it. The old French
officer did it with much less confusion; for leaning a little
over, and nodding to a centinel, and pointing at the
same time with his finger at the distress, the centinel made
his way to it. There was no occasion to tell the grievance
—the thing told itself; so thrusting back the German
instantly with his musket, he took the poor dwarf by the
hand, and placed him before him. This is noble ! said I,
clapping my hands together. And yet you would not
permit this, said the old officer, in England.

In England, dear Sir, said I, *we sit all at our ease*.

The old French officer would have set me at unity with
myself, in case I had been at variance, by saying it was a
bon mot, and as a *bon mot* is always worth something at
Paris, he offered me a pinch of snuff.

THE ROSE—PARIS

It was now my turn to ask the old French officer, "what was the matter?" for a cry of "*Haussez les mains, Monsieur l'Abbé*," re-echoed from a dozen different parts of the parterre, was as unintelligible to me, as my apostrophe to the monk had been to him.

He told me, it was some poor Abbé in one of the upper loges, who he supposed had got planted perdu behind a couple of Grissets in order to see the opera, and that the parterre espying him, were insisting upon his holding up both his hands during the representation. And can it be supposed, said I, that an ecclesiastic would pick the grissets' pockets? The old French officer smiled, and whispering in my ear, opened a door of knowledge which I had no idea of.

Good God! said I, turning pale with astonishment, is it possible, that a people so smit with sentiment should at

the same time be so unclean, and so unlike themselves !
Quelle grossiereté ! added I.

The French officer told me it was an illiberal sarcasm at
the church, which had begun in the theatre about the
time the *Tartuffe* was given in it, by Moliere, but like
other remains of Gothic manners, was declining. Every
nation, continued he, have their refinements and *gros-
sieretés*, in which they take the lead, and lose it of one
another by turns; that he had been in most countries, but
never in one where he found not some delicacies, which
others seemed to want. *Le* POUR *et le* CONTRE *se trouvent
en chaque nation ;* there is a balance, said he, of good and
bad every where; and nothing but the knowing it is so can
emancipate one-half of the world from the prepossession
which it holds against the other; that the advantage of
travel, as it regarded the *sçavoir vivre*, was by seeing a
great deal both of men and manners; it taught us mutual
toleration; and mutual toleration, concluded he, making
me a bow, taught us mutual love.

The old French officer delivered this with an air of such
candour and good sense, as coincided with my first
favourable impressions of his character. I thought I loved
the man; but I fear I mistook the object—'twas my own
way of thinking—the difference was, I could not have
expressed it half so well.

It is alike troublesome to both the rider and his beast
if the latter goes pricking up his ears, and starting all the
way at every object which he never saw before. I have
as little torment of this kind as any creature alive; and
yet I honestly confess, that many a thing gave me pain,
and that I blush'd at many a word the first month which I
found inconsequent and perfectly innocent the second.

Madame de Rambouliet, after an acquaintance of about
six weeks with her, had done me the honour to take me

in her coach about two leagues out of town. Of all women,
Madame de Rambouliet is the most correct; and I never
wish to see one of more virtues and purity of heart. In
our return back, Madame de Rambouliet desired me to
pull the cord. I asked her if she wanted any thing. *Rien
que pisser*, said Madame de Rambouliet.

Grieve not, gentle traveller, to let Madame de Rambouliet p—ss on. And, ye fair mystic nymphs! go each
one *pluck your rose*, and scatter them in your path, for
Madame de Rambouliet did no more. I handed Madame
de Rambouliet out of the coach; and had I been the priest
of the chaste CASTALIA, I could not have served at her
fountain with a more respectful decorum.

THE FILLE DE CHAMBRE—PARIS

What the old French officer had delivered upon travelling, bringing Polonius's advice to his son upon the same subject into my head, and that bringing in Hamlet; and Hamlet, the rest of Shakespeare's works; I stopp'd at the Quai de Conti in my return home, to purchase the whole set.

The bookseller said he had not a set in the world. *Comment!* said I; taking one up out of a set which lay upon the counter betwixt us. He said, they were sent him only to be got bound, and were to be sent back to Versailles in the morning to the Count de B——.

And does the Count de B——, said I, read Shakespeare? *C'est un Esprit fort,* replied the bookseller. He loves English books; and what is more to his honour, Monsieur, he loves the English too. You speak this so civilly, said I, that it is enough to oblige an Englishman to lay out a louis d'or or two at your shop. The book-seller made a bow, and was going to say something, when a young decent girl about twenty, who by her air and dress seemed to be *fille de chambre* to some devout woman of fashion, came into the shop and asked for *Les Egare-ments du Cœur & de l'Esprit*: the bookseller gave her the book directly; she pulled out a little green sattin purse, run round with ribband of the same colour, and putting her finger and thumb into it, she took out the money and paid for it. As I had nothing more to stay me in the shop, we both walk'd out of the door together.

And what have you to do, my dear, said I, with *The Wanderings of the Heart*, who scarce know yet you have one; nor, till love has first told you it, or some faithless shepherd has made it ache, canst thou ever be sure it is so ? *Le Dieu m'en garde !* said the girl. With reason, said I, for if it is a good one, 'tis pity it should be stolen; 'tis a little treasure to thee, and gives a better air to your face, than if it was dress'd out with pearls.

The young girl listened with a submissive attention, holding her sattin purse by its ribband in her hand all the time. 'Tis a very small one, said I, taking hold of the bottom of it—she held it towards me—and there is very little in it, my dear, said I; but be but as good as thou art handsome, and heaven will fill it: I had a parcel of crowns in my hand to pay for Shakespeare; and as she had let go the purse entirely, I put a single one in; and tying up the ribband in a bowknot, returned it to her.

The young girl made me more a humble courtesy than a low one—'twas one of those quiet, thankful sinkings, where the spirit bows itself down; the body does no more than tell it. I never gave a girl a crown in my life which gave me half the pleasure.

My advice, my dear, would not have been worth a pin to you, said I, if I had not given this along with it: but now, when you see the crown, you'll remember it, so don't, my dear, lay it out in ribbands.

Upon my word, Sir, said the girl, earnestly, I am incapable. In saying which, as is usual in little bargains of honour, she gave me her hand: *En verité, Monsieur, je mettrai cet argent apart*, said she.

When a virtuous convention is made betwixt man and woman, it sanctifies their most private walks; so not withstanding it was dusky, yet as both our roads lay the same way, we made no scruple of walking along the Quai de Conti together.

She made me a second courtesy in setting off, and before we got twenty yards from the door, as if she had not done enough before, she made a sort of a little stop to tell me again—she thank'd me.

It was a small tribute, I told her, which I could not avoid paying to virtue, and would not be mistaken in the person I had been rendering it to for the world. But I see innocence, my dear, in your face, and foul befal the man who ever lays a snare in its way!

The girl seem'd affected some way or other with what I said. She gave a low sigh. I found I was not empowered to inquire at all after it, so said nothing more till I got to the corner of the Rue de Nevers, where we were to part.

But is this the way, my dear, said I, to the Hôtel de Modene? She told me it was, or, that I might go by the Rue de Gueneguault, which was the next turn. Then I'll go, my dear, by the Rue de Gueneguault, said I, for two reasons; first I shall please myself, and next I shall give you the protection of my company as far on your way as I can. The girl was sensible I was civil and said, she wish'd the Hôtel de Modene was in the Rue de St. Pierre. You live there? said I. She told me she was *fille de chambre* to Madame R——. Good God! said I, 'tis the very lady for whom I have brought a letter from Amiens. The girl told me that Madame R——, she believed, expected a stranger with a letter, and was impatient to see him. So I desired the girl to present my compliments to Madame R——, and say I would certainly wait upon her in the morning.

We stood still at the corner of the Rue de Nevers whilst this pass'd; we then stopped a moment whilst she disposed of her *Egarements du Cœur*, etc., more commodiously than carrying them in her hand—they were two volumes; so I held the second for her whilst she put the first into her pocket; and then she held her pocket, and I put in the other after it.

'Tis sweet to feel by what fine-spun threads our affections are drawn together.

We set off afresh, and as she took her third step, the girl put her hand within my arm—I was just bidding her—but she did it of herself with that undeliberating simplicity, which show'd it was out of her head that she had never seen me before. For my own part, I felt the conviction of consanguinity so strongly, that I could not help turning half round to look in her face, and see if I could trace out any thing in it of a family likeness. Tut! said I, are we not all relations?

When we arrived at the turning up to the Rue de Gueneguault, I stopp'd to bid her adieu for good and all: the girl would thank me again for my company and kindness. She bid me adieu twice. I repeated it as often; and so cordial was the parting between us, that had it happened any where else, I'm not sure but I should have signed it with a kiss of charity, as warm and holy as an apostle.

But in Paris, as none kiss each other but the men, I did, what amounted to the same thing——

I bid God bless her.

When I got home to my hotel, La Fleur told me I
had been inquired after by the Lieutenant de Police. The
deuce take it! said I; I know the reason. It is time
the reader should know it, for in the order of things in
which it happened, it was omitted; not that it was out
of my head; but that, had I told it then, it might have
been forgot now, and now is the time I want it.

I had left London with so much precipitation, that it
never enter'd my mind that we were at war with France;
and had reached Dover, and looked through my glass at
the hills beyond Boulogne, before the idea presented
itself; and with this in its train, that there was no getting

124

there without a passport. Go but to the end of a street, I have a mortal aversion for returning back no wiser than I set out; and as this was one of the greatest efforts I had ever made for knowledge, I could less bear the thoughts of it; so hearing the Count de —— had hired the packet, I begg'd he would take me in his *suite*. The Count had some little knowledge of me, so made little or no difficulty— only said, his inclination to serve me could reach no further than Calais, as he was to return by way of Brussels to Paris; however, when I had once pass'd there, I might get to Paris without interruption; but that in Paris I must make friends and shift for myself. Let me get to Paris, Monsieur le Count, said I, and I shall do very well. So I embark'd, and never thought more of the matter.

When La Fleur told me the Lieutenant de Police had been inquiring after me the thing instantly recurred, and by the time La Fleur had well told me, the master of the hotel came into my room to tell me the same thing, with this addition to it, that my passport had been particularly asked after: the master of the hotel concluded with saying, He hoped I had one. Not I, faith ! said I.

The master of the hotel retired three steps from me, as from an infected person, as I declared this, and poor La Fleur advanced three steps towards me, and with that sort of movement which a good soul makes to succour a distress'd one. The fellow won my heart by it; and from that single *trait*, I knew his character as perfectly, and could rely upon it as firmly, as if he had served me with fidelity for seven years.

Mon seigneur ! cried the master of the hotel—but recollecting himself as he made the exclamation, he instantly changed the tone of it. If Monsieur, said he, has not a passport, (*apparemment*) in all likelihood he has friends in Paris who can procure him one. Not that I know of, quoth I, with an air of indifference. Then, *certes*, replied he, you'll be sent to the Bastile or the Chatelet, *au moins*. Poo ! said I, the king of France is a good-natur'd soul—he'll hurt nobody. *Cela n'empeche pas*, said he; you will certainly be sent to the Bastile to-morrow morning. But I've taken your lodgings for a month, answer'd I, and I'll not quit them a day before the time for all the kings of France in the world. La Fleur whispered in my ear, That nobody could oppose the king of France.

Pardi ! said my host, *ces Messieurs Anglois sont des gens très extraordinaires ;* and having both said and sworn it, he went out.

I could not find in my heart to torture La Fleur's with a serious look upon the subject of my embarrassment, which was the reason I had treated it so cavalierly; and to shew him how light it lay upon my mind, I dropt the subject entirely; and whilst he waited upon me at supper, talk'd to him with more than usual gaiety about Paris, and of the Opera comique. La Fleur had been there himself, and had followed me through the streets as far as the bookseller's shop; but seeing me come out with the young *fille de chambre*, and that we walk'd down the Quai de Conti together, La Fleur deem'd it unnecessary to follow me a step further, so making his own reflections upon it, he took a shorter cut and got to the hotel in time to be inform'd of the affair of the police against my arrival.

As soon as the honest creature had taken away, and gone down to sup himself, I then began to think a little seriously about my situation.

And here, I know, Eugenius, thou wilt smile at the remembrance of a short dialogue which pass'd betwixt us the moment I was going to set out. I must tell it here.

Eugenius, knowing that I was as little subject to be overburthen'd with money as thought, had drawn me aside to interrogate me how much I had taken care for; upon telling him the exact sum, Eugenius shook his head, and said it would not do; so pull'd out his purse in order to empty it into mine. I've enough in conscience, Eugenius, said I. Indeed, Yorick, you have not, replied Eugenius; I know France and Italy better than you. But you don't consider, Eugenius, said I, refusing his offer, that before I have been three days in Paris, I shall take care to say or do something or other for which I shall get clapp'd up into the Bastile, and that I shall live there a couple of months entirely at the king of France's expense. I beg pardon, said Eugenius, drily: really I had forgot that resource.

Now the event I treated gaily came seriously to my door.

Is it folly, or nonchalance, or philosophy, or pertinacity —or what is it in me, that, after all, when La Fleur had gone downstairs, and I was quite alone, I could not bring down my mind to think of it otherwise than I had then spoken of it to Eugenius?

And as for the Bastile; the terror is in the word. Make the most of it you can, said I to myself, the Bastile is but another word for a tower, and a tower is but another word for a house you can't get out of. Mercy on the gouty! for they are in it twice a year—but with nine livres a day, and pen and ink and paper and patience, albeit a man can't get out, he may do very well within, at least for a month or six weeks; at the end of which, if he is a harmless fellow, his innocence appears, and he comes out a better and wiser man than he went in.

I had some occasion (I forget what) to step into the court-yard, as I settled this account; and remember I walk'd down stairs in no small triumph with the conceit of my reasoning. Beshrew the *sombre* pencil! said I vauntingly, for I envy not its power, which paints the evils of life with so hard and deadly a colouring. The mind sits terrified at the objects she has magnified herself, and blackened: reduce them to their proper size and hue, she overlooks them. 'Tis true, said I, correcting the proposition, the Bastile is not an evil to be despised; but strip it of its towers, fill up the fossé, unbarricade the doors—call it simply a confinement, and suppose 'tis some tyrant of a distemper and not of a man, which holds you in it—the evil vanishes, and you bear the other half without complaint.

I was interrupted in the hey-day of this soliloquy, with a voice which I took to be of a child, which complained "it could not get out." I look'd up and down the passage, and seeing neither man, woman, or child, I went out without further attention.

In my return back through the passage, I heard the same words repeated twice over; and looking up, I saw it was a starling hung in a little cage. "I can't get out; I can't get out," said the starling.

I stood looking at the bird: and to every person who came through the passage it ran fluttering to the side towards which they approach'd it, with the same lamentation of its captivity. "I can't get out," said the starling.

I

God help thee ! said I, but I'll let thee out, cost what it will; so I turned about the cage to get to the door; it was twisted and double twisted so fast with wire, there was no getting it open without pulling the cage to pieces—I took both hands to it.

The bird flew to the place where I was attempting his deliverance, and thrusting his head through the trellis, pressed his breast against it, as if impatient. I fear, poor creature ! said I, I cannot set thee at liberty. "No," said the starling—"I can't get out; I can't get out," said the starling.

I vow I never had my affections more tenderly awakened; or do I remember an incident in my life, where the dissipated spirits, to which my reason had been a bubble, were so suddenly call'd home. Mechanical as the notes were, yet so true in tune to nature were they chaunted, that in one moment they overthrew all my systematic reasonings upon the Bastile; and I heavily walk'd up stairs, unsaying every word I had said in going down them.

Disguise thyself as thou wilt, still, Slavery ! said I, still thou art a bitter draught ! and though thousands in all ages have been made to drink of thee, thou art no less bitter on that account. 'Tis thou, thrice sweet and gracious goddess, addressing myself to LIBERTY, whom all in public or in private worship, whose taste is grateful, and ever will be so, till NATURE herself shall change; no *tint* of words can spot thy snowy mantle, or chymic power turn thy sceptre into iron; with thee to smile upon him as he eats his crust, the swain is happier than his monarch, from whose court thou art exiled. Gracious heaven ! cried I, kneeling down upon the last step but one in my ascent, grant me but health, thou great Bestower of it, and give me but this fair goddess as my companion, and shower down thy mitres, if it seems good unto thy divine providence, upon those heads which are aching for them.

THE CAPTIVE–PARIS

The bird in his cage pursued me into my room; I sat down close to my table, and leaning my head upon my hand, I began to figure to myself the miseries of confinement. I was in a right frame for it, and so I gave full scope to my imagination.

I was going to begin with the millions of my fellow-creatures, born to no inheritance but slavery: but finding, however affecting the picture was, that I could not bring it near me, and that the multitude of sad groups in it did but distract me——

I took a single captive, and having first shut him up in his dungeon, I then look'd through the twilight of his grated door to take his picture.

I beheld his body half wasted away with long expectation and confinement, and felt what kind of sickness of the heart it was which arises from hope deferr'd. Upon looking nearer I saw him pale and feverish: in thirty years the western breeze had not once fann'd his blood; he had seen no sun, no moon, in all that time; nor had the voice of friend or kinsman breathed through his lattice: his children——

But here my heart began to bleed, and I was forced to go on with another part of the portrait.

He was sitting upon the ground upon a little straw, in the furthest corner of his dungeon, which was alternately his chair and bed: a little calendar of small sticks were laid at the head, notch'd all over with the dismal days and nights he had passed there. He had one of these little sticks in his hand, and with a rusty nail he was etching another day of misery to add to the heap. As I darkened the little light he had, he lifted up a hopeless eye towards the door, then cast it down, shook his head, and went on with his work of affliction. I heard his chains upon his legs, as he turned his body to lay his little stick upon the bundle. He gave a deep sigh; I saw the iron enter into his soul. I burst into tears. I could not sustain the picture of confinement which my fancy had drawn. I started up from my chair, and calling La Fleur, I bid him bespeak me a *remise*, and have it ready at the door of the hotel by nine in the morning.

I'll go directly, said I, myself to Monsieur le Duc de Choiseul.

La Fleur would have put me to bed; but not willing he should see any thing upon my cheek which would cost the honest fellow a heart-ache, I told him I would go to bed by myself and bid him go do the same.

THE STARLING—ROAD TO VERSAILLES

I got into my *remise* the hour I promised: La Fleur
got up behind, and I bid the coachman make the best
of his way to Versailles.

As there was nothing in this road, or rather nothing
which I look for in travelling, I cannot fill up the blank
better than with a short history of this self-same bird,
which became the subject of the last chapter.

Whilst the Honourable Mr. —— was waiting for a
wind at Dover, it had been caught upon the cliffs before

it could well fly, by an English lad who was his groom; who not caring to destroy it, had taken it in his breast into the packet, and by course of feeding it, and taking it once under his protection, in a day or two grew fond of it, and got it safe along with him to Paris.

At Paris the lad had laid out a livre in a little cage for the starling, and as he had little to do better the five months his master staid there, he taught it in his mother's tongue the four simple words (and no more) to which I own'd myself so much its debtor.

Upon his master's going on for Italy the lad had given it to the master of the hotel. But his little song for liberty being in an *unknown* language at Paris, the bird had little or no store set by him, so La Fleur bought both him and his cage for me for a bottle of Burgundy.

In my return from Italy I brought him with me to the country in whose language he had learn'd his notes, and telling the story of him to Lord A——, Lord A begg'd the bird of me. In a week Lord A gave him to Lord B——; Lord B made a present of him to Lord C——; and Lord C's gentleman sold him to Lord D's for a shilling. Lord D gave him to Lord E——, and so on—half round the alphabet. From that rank he pass'd into the lower house, and pass'd the hands of as many commoners. But as all these wanted to *get in*, and my bird wanted to *get out*, he had almost as little store set by him in London as in Paris.

It is impossible but many of my readers must have heard of him; and if any by mere chance have ever seen him, I beg leave to inform them, that that bird was my bird or some vile copy set up to represent him.

I have nothing farther to add upon him, but that from that time to this, I have borne this poor starling as the crest to my arms.

And let the heralds' officers twist his neck about if they dare.

THE ADDRESS—VERSAILLES

And let the noblest officers twist his neck about if

I should not like to have my enemy take a view of my mind when I am going to ask protection of any man; for which reason I generally endeavour to protect myself; but this going to Monsieur le Duc de C—— was an act of compulsion. Had it been an act of choice, I should have done it, I suppose, like other people.

How many mean plans of dirty address, as I went along, did my servile heart form ! I deserved the Bastile for every one of them.

Then nothing would serve me, when I got within sight of Versailles, but putting words and sentences together, and conceiving attitudes and tones to wreath myself into Monsieur le Duc de C——'s good graces. This will do, said I. Just as well, retorted I again, as a coat carried up to him by an adventurous tailor, without taking his measure. Fool ! continued I; see Monsieur le Duc's face first.

Observe what character is written in it; take notice in what posture he stands to hear you; mark the turns and expressions of his body and limbs; and for the tone, the first sound which comes from his lips will give it you; and from all these together you'll compound an address at once upon the spot, which cannot disgust the Duke—the ingredients are his own, and most likely to go down.

Well! said I, I wish it well over. Coward again! as if man to man was not equal throughout the whole surface of the globe; and if in the field, why not face to face in the cabinet too? And trust me, Yorick, whenever it is not so, man is false to himself, and betrays his own succours ten times where nature does it once. Go to the Duc de C—— with the Bastile in thy looks—my life for it, thou wilt be sent back to Paris in half an hour with an escort.

I believe so, said I. Then I'll go to the Duke, by Heaven! with all the gaiety and debonairness in the world.

And there you are wrong again, replied I. A heart at ease, Yorick, flies into no extremes—'tis ever on its centre. Well! well! cried I, as the coachman turn'd in at the gates, I find I shall do very well: and by the time he had wheel'd round the court, and brought me up to the door, I found myself so much the better for my own lecture, that I neither ascended the steps like a victim to justice, who was to part with life upon the topmost, nor did I mount them with a skip and a couple of strides, as I do when I fly up, Eliza! to thee, to meet it.

As I entered the door of the saloon, I was met by a person who possibly might be the *maitre d'hôtel*, but had more the air of one of the under-secretaries, who told me the Duc de C—— was busy. I am utterly ignorant, said I, of the forms of obtaining an audience, being an absolute stranger, and what is worse in the present conjuncture of affairs, being an Englishman too. He replied, that did not increase the difficulty. I made him a slight bow, and told him, I had something of importance to say to Monsieur le Duc. The secretary look'd towards the stairs, as if he was about to leave me to carry up this account to some one. But I must not mislead you, said I, for what I have to say is of no manner of importance to Monsieur le Duc de C—— but of great importance to myself. *C'est une autre affaire*, replied he. Not at all, said I, to a man of gallantry. But pray, good Sir, continued I, when can a stranger hope to have *accesse* ? In not less than two hours, said he, looking at his watch. The number of equipages in the court-yard seemed to justify the calculation, that I could have no nearer a prospect, and as walking backwards and forwards in the saloon, without a soul to commune with, was for the time as bad as being in the Bastile itself, I instantly went back to my *remise*, and bid the coachman to drive me to the *Cordon Bleu*, which was the nearest hotel.

I think there is a fatality in it: I seldom go to the place I set out for.

LE PATISSIER–VERSAILLES

Before I had got half-way down the street I changed my mind: as I am at Versailles, thought I, I might as well take a view of the town; so I pull'd the cord, and ordered the coachman to drive round some of the principal streets. I suppose the town is not very large, said I. The coachman begg'd pardon for setting me right, and told me it was very superb, and that numbers of the first dukes and marquises and counts had hotels. The Count de B——, of whom the bookseller at the Quai de Conti had spoken so handsomely the night before, came instantly into my mind. And why should I not go, thought I, to the Count de B——, who has so high an idea of English books and Englishmen—and tell him my story: so I changed my mind a second time. In truth it was the third; for I had intended that day for Madame de R—— in the Rue St. Pierre, and had devoutly sent her word by her *fille de chambre* that I would assuredly wait upon her. But I am governed by circumstances—I cannot govern them: so seeing a man standing with a basket on the other side of the street, as if he had something to sell, I bid La Fleur go up to him and inquire for the Count's hotel.

La Fleur returned a little pale: and told me it was a Chevalier de St. Louis selling *patés*. It is impossible, La Fleur, said I. La Fleur could no more account for the phænomenon than myself; but persisted in his story: he had seen the croix set in gold, with its red ribband, he said, tied to his button-hole, and had looked into the basket and seen the *patés* which the Chevalier was selling; so could not be mistaken in that.

Such a reverse in man's life awakens a better principle than curiosity: I could not help looking for some time at him as I sat in the *remise*. The more I looked at him, his croix, and his basket, the stronger they wove themselves into my brain. I got out of the *remise*, and went towards him.

He was begirt with a clean linen apron, which fell below his knees, and with a sort of a bib that went half-way up his breast; upon the top of this, but a little below the hem, hung his croix. His basket of little *patés* was covered over with a white damask napkin: another of the same kind was spread at the bottom; and there was a look of *propreté* and neatness throughout, that one might have bought his *patés* of him, as much from appetite as sentiment.

He made an offer of them to neither; but stood still with them at the corner of a hotel, for those to buy who chose it, without solicitation.

He was about forty-eight, of a sedate look, something approaching to gravity. I did not wonder. I went up rather to the basket than him, and having lifted up the napkin, and taken one of his *patés* into my hand, I begg'd he would explain the appearance which affected me.

He told me in a few words, that the best part of his life had pass'd in the service, in which, after spending a small patrimony, he had obtain'd a company and the croix with it; but that, at the conclusion of the last peace, his regiment being re-formed, and the whole corps, with those of some other regiments, left without any provision, he found himself in a wide world without friends, without a livre—and indeed, said he, without anything but this (pointing, as he said it, to his croix). The poor Chevalier won my pity, and he finished the scene with winning my esteem too.

The king, he said, was the most generous of princes, but his generosity could neither relieve or reward every one, and it was only his misfortune to be amongst the number. He had a little wife, he said, whom he loved, who did the *patisserie*; and added, he felt no dishonour in defending her and himself from want in this way, unless Providence had offer'd him a better.

It would be wicked to withhold a pleasure from the good, in passing over what happen'd to this poor Chevalier of St. Louis about nine months after.

It seems he usually took his stand near the iron gates which lead up to the palace, and as his croix had caught the eye of numbers, numbers had made the same inquiry which I had done. He had told the same story, and always with so much modesty and good sense, that it had reach'd at last the king's ears, who hearing the Chevalier had been a gallant officer, and respected by the whole regiment as a man of honour and integrity, he broke up his little trade by a pension of fifteen hundred livres a year.

As I have told this to please the reader, I beg he will allow me to relate another, out of its order, to please myself—the two stories reflect light upon each other and 'tis a pity they should be parted.

THE SWORD—RENNES

When states and empires have their periods of declension, and feel in their turns what distress and poverty is—I stop not to tell the causes which gradually brought the house d'E—— in Brittany into decay. The Marquis d'E—— had fought up against his condition with great firmness; wishing to preserve, and still shew to the world, some little fragments of what his ancestors had been; their indiscretions had put it out of his power. There was enough left for the little exigencies of *obscurity*, but he had two boys who look'd up to him for *light*: he thought they deserved it. He had tried his sword—it could not open the way; the *mounting* was too expensive, and simple œconomy was not a match for it. There was no resource but commerce.

In any other province in France, save Brittany, this was

142

smiting the root for ever of the little tree his pride and affection wish'd to see re-blossom. But in Brittany, there being a provision for this, he avail'd himself of it; and taking an occasion when the states were assembled at Rennes, the Marquis, attended with his two boys, entered the court; and having pleaded the right of an ancient law of the duchy, which, though seldom claim'd, he said, was no less in force, he took his sword from his side. Here, said he, take it; and be trusty guardians of it, till better times put me in condition to reclaim it.

The president accepted the Marquis's sword; he staid a few minutes to see it deposited in the archives of his house, and departed.

The Marquis and his whole family embarked the next day for Martinico, and in about nineteen or twenty years of successful application to business, with some unlook'd-for bequests from distant branches of his house, return'd home to reclaim his nobility and to support it.

It was an incident of good fortune which will never happen to any traveller, but a sentimental one, that I should be at Rennes at the very time of this solemn requisition. I call it solemn—it was so to me.

The Marquis enter'd the court with his whole family. He supported his lady, his eldest son supported his sister, and his youngest was at the other extreme of the line next his mother. He put his handkerchief to his face twice.

There was a dead silence. When the Marquis had approach'd within six paces of the tribunal, he gave the Marchioness to his youngest son, and advancing three steps before his family, he reclaim'd his sword. His sword was given him, and the moment he got it into his hand, he drew it almost out of the scabbard—'twas the shining face of a friend he had once given up. He look'd attentively along it, beginning at the hilt, as if to see whether it was the same, when observing a little rust which it had contracted near the point, he brought it near his eye, and bending his head down over it—I think I saw a tear fall upon the place: I could not be deceived by what followed.

"I shall find," said he, "some *other way* to get it off."

When the Marquis had said this, he return'd his sword into its scabbard, made a bow to the guardians of it, and with his wife and daughter, and his two sons following him, walk'd out.

O how I envied him his feelings !

I found no difficulty in getting admittance to Monsieur le Count de B——. The set of Shakespeares was laid upon the table, and he was tumbling them over. I walk'd up close to the table, and giving first such a look at the books as to make him conceive I knew what they were, I told him I had come without any one to present me, knowing I should meet with a friend in his apartment, who, I trusted, would do it for me—it is my countryman the great Shakespeare, said I, pointing to his works. *Et ayez la bonté, mon cher ami*, apostrophising his spirit, added I, *de me faire cet honneur-là.*

The Count smiled at the singularity of the introduction; and seeing I look'd a little pale and sickly, insisted upon my taking an arm-chair; so I sat down; and to save him conjectures upon a visit so out of all rule, I told him simply of the incident in the bookseller's shop, and how that had impelled me rather to go to him with the story of a little embarrassment I was under, than to any other man in France. And what is your embarrassment? let me hear it, said the Count. So I told him the story just as I have told it the reader.

And the master of my hotel, said I, as I concluded it, will needs have it, Monsieur le Count, that I should be sent

K

145

to the Bastile. But I have no apprehensions, continued I, for in falling into the hands of the most polish'd people in the world, and being conscious I was a true man, and not come to spy the nakedness of the land, I scarce thought I laid at their mercy. It does not suit the gallantry of the French, Monsieur le Count, said I, to show it against invalids.

An animated blush came into the Count de B——'s cheeks as I spoke this. *Ne craignez rien*—Don't fear, said he. Indeed I don't, replied I again. Besides, continued I a little sportingly, I have come laughing all the way from London to Paris, and I do not think Monsieur le Duc de Choiseul is such an enemy to mirth, as to send me back crying for my pains.

My application to you, Monsieur le Count de B—— (making him a low bow), is to desire he will not.

The Count heard me with great good-nature, or I had not said half as much, and once or twice said: *C'est bien dit*. So I rested my cause there, and determined to say no more about it.

The Count led the discourse: we talk'd of indifferent things—of books, and politics, and men, and then of women. God bless them all ! said I, after much discourse about them; there is not a man upon earth who loves them so much as I do: after all the foibles I have seen, and all the satires I have read against them, still I love them; being firmly persuaded that a man, who has not a sort of an affection for the whole sex, is incapable of ever loving a single one as he ought.

Heh bien ! Monsieur l' Anglois, said the Count, gaily, you are not come to spy the nakedness of the land—I believe you—*ni encore*, I dare say *that* of our women; but permit me to conjecture: if, *par hazard*, they fell into your way, that the prospect would not affect you.

I have something within me which cannot bear the shock of the least indecent insinuation: in the sportability of chit-chat I have often endeavoured to conquer it, and with infinite pain have hazarded a thousand things to a dozen of the sex together—the least of which I could not venture to a single one to gain heaven.

Excuse me, Monsieur le Count, said I, as for the nakedness of your land, if I saw it, I should cast my eyes over it with tears in them; and for that of your women (blushing at the idea he had excited in me), I am so evangelical in this, and have such a fellow-feeling for whatever is *weak* about them, that I would cover it with a garment, if I knew how to throw it on. But I could wish, continued I, to spy the *nakedness* of their hearts, and through the different disguises of customs, climates, and religion, find out what is good in them to fashion my own by—and therefore am I come.

It is for this reason, Monsieur le Count, continued I, that I have not seen the Palais Royal, nor the Luxembourg, nor the Façade of the Louvre, nor have attempted to swell the catalogues we have of pictures, statues, and churches: I conceive every fair being as a temple, and would rather enter in, and see the original drawings and loose sketches hung up in it, than the transfiguration of Raphael itself.

The thirst of this, continued I, as impatient as that which inflames the breast of the connoisseur, has led me from my own home into France, and from France will lead me through Italy. 'Tis a quiet journey of the heart in pursuit of NATURE, and those affections which arise out of her, which make us love each other, and the world, better than we do.

The Count said a great many civil things to me upon the occasion; and added, very politely, how much he stood obliged to Shakespeare for making me known to him. But, *à-propos*, said he, Shakespeare is full of great things: he forgot a small punctilio of announcing your name—it puts you under a necessity of doing it yourself.

There is not a more perplexing affair in life to me, than to set about telling anyone who I am, for there is scarce any body I cannot give a better account of than myself; and I have often wish'd I could do it in a single word and have an end of it. It was the only time and occasion in my life I could accomplish this to any purpose, for Shakespeare lying upon the table, and recollecting I was in his books, I took up Hamlet, and turning immediately to the grave-diggers' scene in the fifth act, I laid my finger upon YORICK, and advancing the book to the Count, with my finger all the way over the Name—*Me voici !* said I.

Now whether the idea of poor Yorick's skull was put out of the Count's mind by the reality of my own, or by what magic he could drop a period of seven or eight hundred years, makes nothing in this account—'tis

148

certain the French conceive better than they combine
—I wonder at nothing in this world, and the less at this;
inasmuch as one of the first of our own church, for whose
candour and paternal sentiments I have the highest
veneration, fell into the same mistake in the very same case.
"He could not bear," he said, "to look into the sermons
wrote by the king of Denmark's jester." Good my lord !
said I; but there are two Yoricks. The Yorick your lordship thinks of has been dead and buried eight hundred
years ago : he flourish'd in Horwendillus's court; the other
Yorick is myself, who have flourish'd, my lord, in no court.
He shook his head. Good God ! said I, you might as well
confound Alexander the Great with Alexander the Copper-
smith, my lord. 'Twas all one, he replied.

If Alexander king of Macedon could have translated
your lordship, said I, I'm sure your lordship would not
have said so.

The poor Count de B—— fell but into the same *error*.

Et, Monsieur, est-il Yorick? cried the Count. *Je le
suis*, said I. *Vous? Moi—moi qui ai l'honneur de vous
parler, Monsieur le Comte. Mon Dieu !* said he, embracing
me : *Vous êtes Yorick !*

The Count instantly put the Shakespeare into his
pocket, and left me alone in his room.

I could not conceive why the Count de B—— had gone so abruptly out of the room, any more than I could conceive why he had put the Shakespeare into his pocket. *Mysteries which must explain themselves are not worth the loss of time which a conjecture about them takes up*: 'twas better to read Shakespeare; so taking up "*Much ado about Nothing*," I transported myself instantly from the chair I sat in to Messina in Sicily, and got so busy with Don Pedro and Benedict and Beatrice, that I thought not of Versailles, the Count, or the Passport.

Sweet pliability of man's spirit, that can at once surrender itself to illusions, which cheat expectation and sorrow of their weary moments ! Long, long since had he number'd out my days, had I not trod so great a part of them upon this enchanted ground ; when my way is too rough for my feet, or too steep for my strength, I get off it, to some smooth velvet path which fancy has scattered over with rose-buds of delights ; and having taken a few turns in it, come back strengthen'd and refresh'd. When evils press sore upon me, and there is no retreat from them in this world, then I take a new course : I leave it ; and as I have a clearer idea of the elysian fields than I have of heaven, I force myself, like Æneas, into them. I see him meet the pensive shade of his

150

forsaken Dido, and wish to recognise it; I see the injured spirit wave her head, and turn off silent from the author of her miseries and dishonours; I lose the feelings for myself in hers, and in those affections which were wont to make me mourn for her when I was at school.

Surely this is not walking in a vain shadow, nor does man disquiet himself in vain *by it*—he oftener does so in trusting the issue of his commotions to reason only. I can safely say for myself, I was never able to conquer any one single bad sensation in my heart so decisively, as by beating up as fast as I could for some kindly and gentle sensation to fight it upon its own ground.

When I had got to the end of the third act, the Count de B—— entered with my passport in his hand. Mons. le Duc de C——, said the Count, is as good a prophet, I dare say, as he is a statesman. *Un homme qui rit*, said the Duke, *ne sera jamais dangereux*. Had it been for any one but the king's jester, added the Count, I could not have got it these two hours. *Pardonnez moi*, Mons. le Count, said I; I am not the king's jester. But you are Yorick? Yes. *Et vous plaisantez?* I answered: Indeed I did jest—but was not paid for it; 'twas entirely at my own expense.

We have no jester at court, Mons. le Count, said I; the last we had was in the licentious reign of Charles II., since which time our manners have been so gradually refining, that our court at present is so full of patriots, who wish for *nothing* but the honours and wealth of their country; and our ladies are all so chaste, so spotless, so good, so devout, there is nothing for a jester to make a jest of.

Voila un persiflage ! cried the Count.

THE PASSPORT ~ VERSAILLES

As the Passport was directed to all lieutenant-governors, governors, and commandants of cities, generals or armies, justiciaries, and all officers of justice, to let Mr. Yorick, the king's jester, and his baggage, travel quietly along, I own the triumph of obtaining the Passport was not a little tarnish'd by the figure I cut in it. But there is nothing unmix'd in this world; and some of the gravest of our divines have carried it so far as to affirm, that enjoyment itself was attended even with a sigh, and that the greatest *they knew of* terminated *in a general way,* in little better than a convulsion.

I remember the grave and learned Bevoriskius, in his Commentary upon the Generations from Adam, very naturally breaks off in the middle of a note to give an account to the world of a couple of sparrows upon the

152

out-edge of his window, which had incommoded him all the time he wrote, and at last had entirely taken him off from his genealogy.

'Tis strange ! writes Bevoriskius, but the facts are certain, for I have had the curiosity to mark them down one by one with my pen, but the cock-sparrow, during the little time that I could have finished the other half of this note, has actually interrupted me with the reiteration of his caresses three-and-twenty times and a half.

How merciful, adds Bevoriskius, is heaven to his creatures !

Ill-fated Yorick ! that the gravest of thy brethren should be able to write that to the world, which stains thy face with crimson, to copy in even thy study.

But this is nothing to my travels. So I twice—twice beg pardon for it.

CHARACTER—VERSAILLES

And how do you find the French? said the Count de B——, after he had given me the Passport.

The reader may suppose, that after so obliging a proof of courtesy, I could not be at a loss to say something handsome to the inquiry.

Mais passe, pour cela; Speak frankly, said he: do you find all the urbanity in the French which the world gives us the honour of? I had found every thing, I said, which confirmed it. *Vraiment*, said the Count; *les François sont polis*. To an excess, replied I.

The Count took notice of the word *excess*; and would have it I meant more than I said. I defended myself a long time as well as I could against it; he insisted I had a reserve, and that I would speak my opinion frankly.

I believe, Mons. le Count, said I, that man has a certain compass, as well as an instrument; and that the social and other calls have occasion by turns for every key in him; so that if you begin a note too high or too low, there must be a want in the upper or under part, to fill up the system of harmony. The Count de B—— did not understand music, so desired me to explain it some other way. A polish'd nation, my dear Count, said I, makes every one its debtor; and besides, urbanity itself, like the fair sex, has so many charms, it goes against the heart to say it can do ill; and yet, I believe, there is but a certain line of perfection, that man, take him altogether, is impower'd to arrive at—if he gets beyond, he rather exchanges qualities than gets them. I must not presume to say, how far this has affected the French in the subject we are speaking of, but should it ever be the case of the English, in the progress of their refinements, to arrive at the same polish which distinguishes the French, if we did not lose the *politesse de cœur*, which inclines men more to humane actions than courteous ones, we should at least lose that distinct variety and originality of character, which distinguishes them, not only from each other, but from all the world besides.

I had a few of King William's shillings as smooth as glass in my pocket; and foreseeing they would be of use in the illustration of my hypothesis, I had got them into my hand, when I had proceeded so far.

See, Mons. le Count, said I, rising up, and laying them before him upon the table; by jingling and rubbing one against another for seventy years together in one body's pocket or another's, they are become so much alike, you can scarce distinguish one shilling from another.

The English, like ancient medals, kept more apart, and passing but few people's hands, preserve the first sharpnesses which the fine hand of Nature has given them: they are not so pleasant to feel, but, in return, the legend is so visible, that at the first look you see whose image and superscription they bear. But the French, Mons. le Count, added I (wishing to soften what I had said), have so many excellencies, they can the better spare this: they are a loyal, a gallant, a generous, an ingenious, and good-temper'd people as is under heaven; if they have a fault, they are too *serious*.

Mon Dieu ! cried the Count, rising out of his chair.

Mais vous plaisantez, said he, correcting his exclamation. I laid my hand upon my breast, and with earnest gravity assured him it was my most settled opinion.

The Count said he was mortified he could not stay to hear my reasons, being engaged to go that moment to dine with the Duc de C——.

But if it is not too far to come to Versailles to eat your soup with me, I beg, before you leave France, I may have the pleasure of knowing you retract your opinion, or, in what manner you support it. But if you do support it, Mons. Anglois, said he, you must do it with all your powers, because you have the whole world against you. I promised the Count I would do myself the honour of dining with him before I set out for Italy; so took my leave.

THE TEMPTATION—PARIS

When I alighted at the hotel, the porter told me a young woman with a bandbox had been that moment enquiring for me. I do not know, said the porter, whether she is gone away or no. I took the key of my chamber of him, and went up stairs; and when I had got within ten steps of the top of the landing before my door, I met her coming easily down.

It was the fair *fille de chambre* I had walked along the Quai de Conti with: Madame de R—— had sent her upon some commisson to a *merchande de modes* within a step or two of the Hotel de Modene; and as I had fail'd in waiting upon her, had bid her enquire if I had left Paris; and if so, whether I had not left a letter addressed to her.

As the fair *fille de chambre* was so near my door, she returned back, and went into the room with me for a moment or two while I wrote a card.

It was a fine still evening in the latter end of the month of May. The crimson window-curtains (which were of the same colour as those of the bed) were drawn close; the sun was setting, and reflected through them so warm a tint into the fair *fille de chambre's* face, I thought she blush'd—the idea of it made me blush myself. We were quite alone; and that superinduced a second blush before the first could get off.

There is a sort of a pleasing half-guilty blush, where the blood is more in fault than the man : 'tis sent impetuous from the heart, and virtue flies after it—not to call it back, but to make the sensation of it more delicious to the nerves—'tis associated.

But I'll not describe it. I felt something at first within me which was not in strict unison with the lesson of virtue I had given her the night before. I sought five minutes for a card; I knew I had not one. I took up a pen, I laid it down again; my hand trembled, the devil was in me.

I know as well as any one he is an adversary, whom if we resist he will fly from us. But I seldom resist him at all, from a terror that though I may conquer, I may still get a hurt in the combat—so I give up the triumph for security; and instead of thinking to make him fly, I generally fly myself.

The fair *fille de chambre* came close up to the bureau where I was looking for a card, took up first the pen I cast down, then offer'd to hold me the ink; she offer'd it so sweetly, I was going to accept it—but I durst not. I have nothing, my dear, said I, to write upon. Write it, said she, simply, upon any thing.

I was just going to cry out, Then I will write it, fair girl ! upon thy lips.

If I do, said I, I shall perish—so I took her by the hand, and led her to the door, and begg'd she would not forget the lesson I had given her. She said, indeed she would not; and as she uttered it with some earnestness, she turn'd about, and gave me both her hands, closed together, into mine. It was impossible not to compress them in that situation. I wished to let them go; and all the time I held them, I kept arguing within myself against it—and still I held them on. In two minutes I found I had all the battle to fight over again, and I felt my legs and every limb tremble at the idea.

The foot of the bed was within a yard and a half of the place where we were standing; I had still hold of her hands; and how it happened I can give no account, but I neither ask'd her, nor drew her, nor did I think of the bed, but so it did happen, we both sat down.

I'll just show you, said the fair *fille de chambre*, the little purse I have been making to-day to hold your crown. So she put her hand into her right pocket, which was next me, and felt for it some time, then into the left—"She had lost it." I never bore expectation more quietly. It was in her right pocket at last—she pull'd it out. It was of green taffeta, lined with a little bit of white quilted sattin, and just big enough to hold the crown. She put it into my hand; it was pretty; and I held it ten minutes with the back of my hand resting upon her lap, looking sometimes at the purse, sometimes on one side of it.

A stitch or two had broke out in the gathers of my stock. The fair *fille de chambre*, without saying a word, took out her little housewife, threaded a small needle, and sew'd it up. I foresaw it would hazard the glory of the day; and as she pass'd her hand in silence across and across my neck in the manœuvre, I felt the laurels shake which fancy had wreath'd about my head.

A strap had given way in her walk, and the buckle of her shoe was just falling off. See, said the *fille de chambre*, holding up her foot. I could not from my soul but fasten the buckle in return; and putting in the strap, and lifting up the other foot with it, when I had done, to see both were right—in doing it too suddenly it unavoidably threw the fair *fille de chambre* off her centre, and then——

THE CONQUEST

Yes—and then—— Ye whose clay-cold heads and lukewarm hearts can argue down or mask your passions, tell me, what trespass is it that man should have them? or how his spirit stands answerable to the Father of spirits but for his conduct under them.

If Nature has so wove her web of kindness that some threads of love and desire are entangled with the piece, must the whole web be rent in drawing them out? Whip me such stoics, great Governor of nature! said I to myself. Wherever thy providence shall place me for the trials of my virtue, whatever is my danger, whatever is my situation, let me feel the movements which rise out of it, and which belong to me as a man—and if I govern them as a good one, I will trust the issues to thy justice: for thou hast made us, and not we ourselves.

As I finish'd my address, I raised the fair *fille de chambre* up by the hand, and led her out of the room. She stood by me till I lock'd the door and put the key in my pocket— —*and then*—the victory being quite decisive, and not till then, I press'd my lips to her cheek, and taking her by the hand again, led her safe to the gate of the hotel.

THE MYSTERY~PARIS

If a man knows the heart, he will know it was impossible to go back instantly to my chamber: it was touching a cold key with a flat third to it, upon the close of a piece of music, which had call'd forth my affections. Therefore when I let go the hand of the *fille de chambre*, I remain'd at the gate of the hotel for some time, looking at every one who pass'd by, and forming conjectures upon them, till my attention got fix'd upon a single object which confounded all kind of reasoning upon him.

It was a tall figure of a philosophic, serious, adult look, which pass'd and repass'd sedately along the street, making a turn of about sixty paces on each side of the gate of the hotel. The man was about fifty-two, had a small cane under his arm, was dress'd in a dark drab-coloured coat, waistcoat, and breeches, which seem'd to have seen some years' service—they were still clean, and there was a little air of frugal *propreté* throughout him. By his pulling off his hat, and his attitude of accosting a good many in his way, I saw he was asking charity; so I got a sous or two out of my pocket ready to give him, as he took me in his turn. He pass'd by me without asking any thing, and yet did not go five steps farther before he ask'd charity of a little woman—I was much more likely to have given of the two. He had scarce done with the woman, when he pull'd his hat off to another who was coming the same way. An ancient gentleman came slowly, and, after him, a young smart one. He let them both pass, and ask'd nothing; I stood observing him half an hour, in which time he had made a dozen turns backwards and forwards, and found that he invariably pursued the same plan.

There were two things very singular in this, which set my brain to work, and to no purpose: the first was, why the man should *only* tell his story to the sex; and secondly, what kind of story it was, and what species of eloquence it could be, which soften'd the hearts of the women, which he knew 'twas to no purpose to practise upon the men.

There were two other circumstances which entangled this mystery: the one was, he told every woman what he had to say in her ear, and in a way which had much more the air of a secret than a petition; the other was, it was always successful—he never stopp'd a woman, but she pull'd out her purse, and immediately gave him something.

I could form no system to explain the phænomenon.

I had got a riddle to amuse me for the rest of the evening, so I walk'd up stairs to my chamber.

I was immediately followed up by the master of the hotel, who came into my room to tell me I must provide lodgings elsewhere. How so, friend? said I. He answer'd, I had had a young woman lock'd up with me two hours that evening in my bed-chamber, and 'twas against the rules of his house. Very well, said I, we'll all part friends then; for the girl is no worse, and I am no worse, and you will be just as I found you. It was enough, he said, to overthrow the credit of his hotel. *Voyez vous, Monsieur*, said he, pointing to the foot of the bed we had been sitting upon. I own it had something of the appearance of an evidence; but my pride not suffering me to enter into any detail of the case, I exhorted him to let his soul sleep in peace, as I resolved to let mine do that night, and that I would discharge what I owed him at breakfast.

I should not have minded, *Monsieur*, said he, if you had had twenty girls—'Tis a score more, replied I, interrupting him, than I ever reckon'd upon—Provided, added he, it had been but in a morning. And does the difference of the time of the day at Paris make a difference in the sin ? It made a difference, he said, in the scandal. I like a good distinction in my heart; and cannot say I was intolerably out of temper with the man. I own it is necessary, reassumed the master of the hotel, that a stranger at Paris should have the opportunities presented to him of buying lace and silk stockings, and ruffles, *et tout cela*, and 'tis nothing if a woman comes with a bandbox. O' my conscience, said I, she had one; but I never look'd into it. Then *Monsieur*, said he, has bought nothing. Not one earthly thing, replied I. Because, said he, I could recommend one to you who would use you *en conscience*. But I must see her this night, said I. He made me a low bow, and walk'd down.

Now, shall I triumph over this *maître d'hôtel*, cried I—and what then ? Then I shall let him see I know he is a dirty fellow. And what then ? What then ? I was too near myself to say it was for the sake of others. I had no good answer left: there was more of spleen than principle in my project, and I was sick of it before the execution.

In a few minutes the Grisset came in with her box of lace. I'll buy nothing, however, said I, within myself.

The Grisset would show me every thing. I was hard to please: she would not seem to see it; she open'd her little magazine, and laid all her laces one after another before me, unfolded and folded them up again one by one with the most patient sweetness. I might buy or not, she would let me have every thing at my own price; the poor creature seem'd anxious to get a penny; and laid herself out to win me, and not so much in a manner which seem'd artful, as in one I felt simple and caressing.

If there is not a fund of honest cullibility in man, so much the worse: my heart relented, and I gave up my second resolution as quietly as the first. Why should I chastise one for the trespass of another? If thou art tributary to this tyrant of an host, thought I, looking up in her face, so much harder is thy bread.

If I had not had more than four louis d'ors in my purse, there was no such thing as rising up and showing her the door, till I had first laid three of them out in a pair of ruffles.

The master of the hotel will share the profit with her. No matter! then I have paid only as many a poor soul has *paid* before me, for an act he *could* not do, or think of.

THE RIDDLE - PARIS

When La Fleur came up to wait upon me at supper, he told me how sorry the master of the hotel was for his affront to me in bidding me change my lodgings.

A man who values a good night's rest will not lie down with enmity in his heart, if he can help it, so I bid La Fleur tell the master of the hotel, that I was sorry on my side for the occasion I had given him; and you may tell him, if you will, La Fleur, added I, that if the young woman should call again, I shall not see her.

This was a sacrifice not to him, but myself, having resolved, after so narrow an escape, to run no more risks, but to leave Paris, if it was possible, with all the virtue I enter'd it.

C'est deroger à noblesse, Monsieur, said La Fleur, making me a bow down to the ground as he said it. *Et encore, Monsieur,* said he, may change his sentiments;

and if (*par hazard*) he should like to amuse himself—I find no amusement in it, said I, interrupting him.

Mon Dieu ! said La Fleur—and took away.

In an hour's time he came to put me to bed, and was more than commonly officious: something hung upon his lips to say to me, or ask me, which he could not get off: I could not conceive what it was, and indeed gave myself little trouble to find it out, as I had another riddle so much more interesting upon my mind, which was that of the man's asking charity before the door of the hotel. I would have given any thing to have got to the bottom of it; and that, not out of curiosity—'tis so low a principle of inquiry, in general, I would not purchase the gratification of it with a two-sous piece—but a secret, I thought, which so soon and so certainly soften'd the heart of every woman you came near, was a secret at last equal to the philosopher's stone: had I had both the Indies, I would have given up one to have been master of it.

I toss'd and turn'd it almost all night long in my brains to no manner of purpose; and when I awoke in the morning, I found my spirit as much troubled with my *dreams*, as ever the king of Babylon had been with his; and I will not hesitate to affirm, it would have puzzled all the wise men of Paris as much as those of Chaldea, to have given its interpretation.

LE DIMANCHE ~ PARIS

It was Sunday; and when La Fleur came in, in the morning, with my coffee and roll and butter, he had got himself so gallantly array'd, I scarce knew him.

I had covenanted at Montriul to give him a new hat with a silver button and loop, and four louis d'ors *pour s'adoniser*, when we got to Paris; and the poor fellow, to do him justice, had done wonders with it.

He had bought a bright, clean, good scarlet coat, and a pair of breeches of the same—they were not a crown worse, he said, for the wearing. I wish'd him hang'd for telling me—they look'd so fresh, that tho' I knew the thing could not be done, yet I would rather have imposed upon my fancy with thinking I had bought them new for the fellow, than that they had come out of the *Rue de Friperie*.

This is a nicety which makes not the heart sore at Paris.

He had purchased moreover a handsome blue sattin waistcoat, fancifully enough embroidered. This was indeed something the worse for the service it had done, but 'twas clean scour'd, the gold had been touch'd up, and upon the whole was rather showy than otherwise; and as the blue was not violent, it suited with the coat and breeches very well. He had squeez'd out of the money, moreover, a new bag and a solitaire; and had insisted with the *fripier* upon a gold pair of garters to his breeches knees. He had purchased muslin ruffles *bien brodées*, with four livres of his own money and a pair of white silk stockings for five more; and, to top all, nature had given him a handsome figure, without costing him a sous.

He entered the room thus set off, with his hair drest in the first style, and with a handsome *bouquet* in his breast—in a word, there was that look of festivity in every thing about him, which at once put me in mind it was Sunday, and by combining both together, it instantly struck me, that the favour he wish'd to ask of me the night before, was to spend the day as every body in Paris spent it besides. I had scarce made the conjecture, when La Fleur, with infinite humility, but with a look of trust, as if I should not refuse him, begg'd I would grant him the day, *pour faire le galant vis-à-vis de sa maitresse.*

Now it was the very thing I intended to do myself *vis-à-vis* Madame de R——. I had retained the *remise* on purpose for it, and it would not have mortified my vanity to have had a servant so well dress'd as La Fleur was, to have got up behind it: I never could have worse spared him.

But we must *feel*, not argue, in these embarrassments. The sons and daughters of service part with liberty, but not with nature, in their contracts; they are flesh and blood, and have their little vanities and wishes in the midst of the house of bondage, as well as their task-masters. No doubt they have set their self-denials at a price, and their expectations are so unreasonable, that I would often disappoint them, but that their condition puts it so much in my power to do it.

Behold, Behold, I am thy servant ! disarms me at once of the powers of a master.

Thou shalt go, La Fleur ! said I.

And what mistress, La Fleur, said I, canst thou have pick'd up in so little a time at Paris ? La Fleur laid his hand upon his breast, and said 'twas a *petite demoiselle*, at Monsieur le Count de B——'s. La Fleur had a heart made for society; and, to speak the truth of him, let as few occasions slip him as his master—so that somehow or other, but how Heaven knows—he had connected himself with the *demoiselle* upon the landing of the staircase, during the time I was taken up with my passport; and as there was time enough for me to win the Count to my interest, La Fleur had contrived to make it do to win the maid to his. The family, it seems, was to be at Paris that day, and he had made a party with her, and two or three more of the Count's household, upon the *boulevards*.

Happy people ! that once a week at least are sure to lay down all your cares together, and dance and sing, and sport away the weights of grievance, which bow down the spirit of other nations to the earth.

THE FRAGMENT—PARIS

La Fleur had left me something to amuse myself with for the day more than I had bargain'd for, or could have entered either into his head or mine.

He had brought the little print of butter upon a currant-leaf; and as the morning was warm, he had begg'd a sheet of waste paper to put betwixt the currant-leaf and his hand. As that was plate sufficient, I bade him lay it upon the table as it was; and as I resolved to stay within all day, I ordered him to call upon the *traiteur* to bespeak my dinner, and leave me to breakfast by myself.

When I had finished the butter, I threw the currant-leaf out of the window, and was going to do the same by the waste paper, but stopping to read a line first, and that drawing me on to a second and third, I thought it better worth; so I shut the window, and drawing a chair up to it, I sat down to read it.

It was in the old French of Rabelais's time, and for aught I know might have been wrote by him; it was moreover in a Gothic letter, and that so faded and gone off by damps and length of time, it cost me infinite trouble to make any thing of it. I threw it down; and then wrote a letter to Eugenius. Then I took it up again and embroiled my patience with it afresh—and then to cure that, I wrote a letter to Eliza. Still it kept hold of me; and the difficulty of understanding it increased but the desire.

I got my dinner; and after I had enlightened my mind with a bottle of Burgundy, I at it again, and after two or three hours poring upon it, with almost as deep attention as ever Gruter or Jacob Spon did upon a nonsensical inscription, I thought I made sense of it. But to make sure of it, the best way, I imagined, was to turn it into English, and see how it would look then—so I went on leisurely as a trifling man does, sometimes writing a sentence, then taking a turn or two, and then looking how the world went out of the window; so that it was nine o'clock at night before I had done it. I then began and read it as follows.

Now as the Notary's wife disputed the point with the Notary with too much heat—I wish, said the Notary (throwing down the parchment), that there was another Notary here only to set down and attest all this.

And what would you do then, Monsieur? said she, rising hastily up. The Notary's wife was a little fume of a woman, and the Notary thought it well to avoid a hurricane by a mild reply. I would go, answered he, to bed. You may go to the devil, answer'd the Notary's wife.

Now there happening to be but one bed in the house, the other two rooms being unfurnished, as is the custom at Paris, and the Notary not caring to lie in the same bed with a woman who had but that moment sent him pellmell to the devil, went forth with his hat and cane and short cloak, the night being very windy, and walk'd out ill at ease towards the *Pont Neuf*.

Of all the bridges which ever were built, the whole world who have pass'd over the *Pont Neuf* must own, that it is the noblest, the finest, the grandest, the lightest, the longest, the broadest that ever conjoin'd land and land together upon the face of the terraqueous globe.

By this it seems as if the author of the fragment had not been a Frenchman.

The worst fault which divines and the doctors of the Sorbonne can allege against it, is, that if there is but a cap-full of wind in or about Paris, 'tis more blasphemously *sacré Dieu*'d there than in any other aperture of the whole city—and with reason, good and cogent, Messieurs; for it comes against you without crying *garde d'eau*, and with such unpremeditable puffs, that of the few who cross it with their hats on, not one in fifty but hazards two livres and a half, which is its full worth.

The poor Notary, just as he was passing by the sentry, instinctively clapp'd his cane to the side of it, but in raising it up, the point of his cane catching hold of the loop of the centinel's hat, hoisted it over the spikes of the ballustrade clear into the Seine.

'Tis an ill wind, said a boatman, who catch'd it, *which blows nobody any good.*

The sentry, being a Gascon, incontinently twirl'd up his whiskers, and levell'd his harquebuss.

Harquebusses in those days went off with matches; and an old woman's paper lantern at the end of the bridge happening to be blown out, she had borrow'd the sentry's match to light it. It gave a moment's time for the Gascon's blood to run cool, and turn the accident better to his advantage. *'Tis an ill wind*, said he, catching off the Notary's castor, and legitimating the capture with the boatman's adage.

The poor Notary cross'd the bridge, and passing along the rue de Dauphine into the fauxbourgs of St. Germain, lamented himself as he walked along in this manner:

Luckless man that I am ! said the Notary, to be the sport of hurricanes all my days, to be born to have the storm of ill language levell'd against me and my profession wherever I go, to be forced into marriage by the thunder of the church to a tempest of a woman, to be driven forth out of my house by domestic winds, and despoil'd of my castor by pontific ones, to be here, bare-headed, in a windy night at the mercy of the ebbs and flows of accidents. Where am I to lay my head ? Miserable man ! what wind in the two-and-thirty points of the whole compass can blow unto thee, as it does to the rest of thy fellow-creatures, good !

As the Notary was passing on by a dark passage, complaining in this sort, a voice call'd out to a girl, to bid her run for the next Notary. Now the Notary being the next, and availing himself of his situation, walk'd up the passage to the door, and passing through an old sort of a saloon, was usher'd into a large chamber, dismantled of every thing but a long military pike, a breast-plate, a rusty old sword, and bandoleer, hung up equidistant in four different places against the wall.

An old personage, who had heretofore been a gentleman, and unless decay of fortune taints the blood along with it, was a gentleman at that time, lay supporting his head upon his hand, in his bed; a little table with a taper burning was set close beside it, and close by the table was placed a chair. The Notary sat him down in it; and pulling out his inkhorn and a sheet or two of paper which he had in his pocket, he placed them before him, and dipping his pen in his ink, and leaning his breast over the table, he disposed every thing to make the gentleman's last will and testament.

Alas ! Monsieur le Notaire, said the gentleman, raising himself up a little, I have nothing to bequeath which will

pay the expence of bequeathing, except the history of
myself, which I could not die in peace unless I left it as a
legacy to the world; the profits arising out of it I bequeath
to you for the pains of taking it from me. It is a story so
uncommon, it must be read by all mankind; it will make
the fortunes of your house. The Notary dipp'd his pen
into his inkhorn. Almighty Director of every event in
my life ! said the old gentleman, looking up earnestly,
and raising his hands towards heaven; Thou, whose hand
hast led me on through such a labyrinth of strange passages down into this scene of desolation, assist the decaying
memory of an old, infirm, and broken-hearted man; direct
my tongue by the spirit of thy eternal truth, that this
stranger may set down nought but what is written in that
Book, from whose records, said he, clasping his hands
together, I am to be condemn'd or acquitted ! The
Notary held up the point of his pen betwixt the taper and
his eye.

M

It is a story, Monsieur le Notaire, said the gentleman, which will rouse up every affection in nature; it will kill the humane, and touch the heart of cruelty herself with pity——

The Notary was inflamed with a desire to begin, and put his pen a third time into his inkhorn, and the old gentleman turning a little more towards the Notary, began to dictate his story in these words——

And where is the rest of it, La Fleur? said I; he just then entered the room.

THE FRAGMENT & THE BOUQUET—PARIS

When La Fleur came up close to the table, and was made to comprehend what I wanted, he told me there were only two other sheets of it, which he had wrapt round the stalks of a *bouquet* to keep it together, which he had presented to the *demoiselle* upon the *boulevards*. Then prithee, La Fleur, said I, step back to her to the Count de B——'s hotel, and *see if you can get*——There is no doubt of it, said La Fleur, and away he flew.

In a very little time the poor fellow came back quite out of breath, with deeper marks of disappointment in his looks than could arise from the simple irreparability of the fragment. *Juste ciel !* in less than two minutes that the poor fellow had taken his last tender farewell of her, his faithless mistress had given his *gage d'amour* to one of the Count's footmen, the footman to a young sempstress, and the sempstress to a fidler, with my fragment at the end of it. Our misfortunes were involved together: I gave a sigh, and La Fleur echo'd it back again to my ear.

How perfidious ! cried La Fleur. How unlucky ! said I.

I should not have been mortified, Monsieur, quoth La Fleur, if she had lost it. Nor I, La Fleur, said I, had I found it.

Whether I did or no will be seen hereafter.

¹ Nosegay.

179

The man who either disdains or fears to walk up a
dark entry, may be an excellent good man, and fit for
a hundred things; but he will not do to make a good
sentimental traveller. I count little of the many things
I see pass at broad noon-day, in large and open streets.
Nature is shy, and hates to act before spectators; but in
such an unobserved corner you sometimes see a single
short scene of hers, worth all the sentiments of a dozen
French plays compounded together. And yet they are
absolutely fine; and whenever I have a more brilliant affair
upon my hands than common, as they suit a preacher just
as well as a hero, I generally make my sermon out of 'em,
and for the text: "Cappadocia, Pontus and Asia, Phrygia
and Pamphylia " is as good as any one in the Bible.

There is a long dark passage issuing out from the Opera
comique into a narrow street; 'tis trod by a few who

humbly wait for a *fiacre*,[1] or wish to get off quietly o'foot when the opera is done. At the end of it, towards the theatre, 'tis lighted by a small candle, the light of which is almost lost before you get half-way down, but near the door. 'Tis more for ornament than use: you see it as a fix'd star of the least magnitude; it burns, but does little good to the world, that we know of.

In returning along this passage, I discern'd, as I approach'd within five or six paces of the door, two ladies standing arm in arm with their backs against the wall, waiting, as I imagined, for a *fiacre*. As they were next the door, I thought they had a prior right; so edged myself up within a yard or little more of them and quietly took my stand. I was in black, and scarce seen.

The lady next me was a tall lean figure of a woman, of about thirty-six; the other of the same size and make, of about forty. There was no mark of wife or widow in any one part of either of them: they seem'd to be two upright vestal sisters, unsapp'd by caresses, unbroke in upon by tender salutations. I could have wish'd to have made them happy—their happiness was destin'd, that night, to come from another quarter.

A low voice, with a good turn of expression, and sweet cadence at the end of it, begg'd for a twelve-sous piece betwixt them, for the love of Heaven. I thought it singular that a beggar should fix the quota of an alms, and that the sum should be twelve times as much as what is usually given in the dark. They both seem'd astonish'd at it as much as myself. Twelve sous ! said one. A twelve-sous piece ! said the other, and made no reply.

The poor man said, he knew not how to ask less of ladies of their rank; and bow'd down his head to the ground.

Poo ! said they; we have no money.

[1] Hackney-coach.

The beggar remained silent for a moment or two, and renew'd his supplication.

Do not, my fair young ladies, said he, stop your good ears against me. Upon my word, honest man ! said the younger, we have no change. Then God bless you, said the poor man, and multiply those joys which you can give to others without change ! I observed the elder sister put her hand into her pocket. I'll see, said she, if I have a sous. A sous ! give twelve, said the supplicant; Nature has been bountiful to you, be bountiful to a poor man.

I would, friend, with all my heart, said the younger, if I had it.

My fair charitable ! said he, addressing himself to the elder; what is it but your goodness and humanity which makes your bright eyes so sweet, that they outshine the morning even in this dark passage ? and what was it which made the Marquis de Santerre and his brother say so much of you both as they just pass'd by ?

The two ladies seemed much affected; and impulsively at the same time they both put their hands into their pocket, and each took out a twelve-sous piece.

The contest betwixt them and the poor supplicant was no more: it was continued betwixt themselves, which of the two should give the twelve-sous piece in charity, and to end the dispute, they both gave it together, and the man went away.

I stepped hastily after him: it was the very man whose success in asking charity of the women before the door of the hotel had so puzzled me, and I found at once his secret, or at least the basis of it—'twas flattery.

Delicious essence! how refreshing art thou to nature! how strongly are all its powers and all its weaknesses on thy side! how sweetly dost thou mix with the blood, and help it through the most difficult and tortuous passages to the heart!

The poor man, as he was not straiten'd for time, had given it here in a larger dose: 'tis certain he had a way of bringing it into less form, for the many sudden cases he had to do with in the streets; but how he contrived to correct, sweeten, concenter, and qualify it, I vex not my spirit with the inquiry—it is enough, the beggar gained two twelve-sous pieces, and they can best tell the rest, who have gained much greater matters by it.

PARIS

We get forwards in the world, not so much by doing services, as receiving them; you take a withering twig, and put it in the ground; and then you water it because you have planted it.

Mons. le Count de B——, merely because he had done me one kindness in the affair of my passport, would go on and do me another, the few days he was at Paris, in making me known to a few people of rank; and they were to present me to others, and so on.

I had got master of my *secret* just in time to turn these honours to some little account; otherwise, as is commonly the case, I should have din'd or supp'd a single time or two round, and then by *translating* French looks and attitudes into plain English, I should presently have seen that I had gold out of the *couvert*[1] of some more entertaining guest; and in course should have resigned all my places one after another, merely upon the principle that I could not keep them. As it was, things did not go much amiss.

[1] Plate, napkin, knife, fork, and spoon.

I had the honour of being introduced to the old Marquis de B——: in days of yore he had signaliz'd himself by some small feats of chivalry in the *Cour d'amour*, and had dress'd himself out to the idea of tilts and tournaments ever since— the Marquis de B—— wish'd to have it thought the affair was somewhere else than in his brain. "He could like to take a trip to England," and ask'd much of the English ladies. Stay where you are, I beseech you, Mons. le Marquis, said I; Les Messrs. Angloise can scarce get a kind look from them as it is. The Marquis invited me to supper.

Mons. P—— the farmer-general was just as inquisitive about our taxes. They were very considerable, he heard. If we knew but how to collect them, said I, making him a low bow.

I could never have been invited to Mons. P——'s concerts upon any other terms.

I had been misrepresented to Madame de Q—— as an *esprit*. Madame de Q—— was an *esprit* herself: she burnt with impatience to see me, and hear me talk. I had not taken my seat, before I saw she did not care a sous whether I had any wit or no—I was let in, to be convinced she had. I call Heaven to witness I never once open'd the door of my lips.

Madame de V—— vow'd to every creature she met, "She had never had a more improving conversation with a man in her life."

There are three epochas in the empire of a French woman: She is coquette, then deist, then *devôte*. The empire during these is never lost—she only changes her subjects. When thirty-five years and more have unpeopled her dominions of the slaves of love, she repeoples it with slaves of infidelity, and then with the slaves of the church.

Madame de V—— was vibrating betwixt the first of

these epochas: the colour of the rose was fading fast away—she ought to have been a deist years before the time I had the honour to pay my first visit.

She placed me upon the same sopha with her, for the sake of disputing the point of religion more closely: In short, Madame de V—— told me she believed nothing.

I told Madame de V—— it might be her principle; but I was sure it could not be her interest to level the outworks, without which I could not conceive how such a citadel as hers could be defended—that there was not a more dangerous thing in the world than for a beauty to be a deist; that it was a debt I owed my creed, not to conceal it from her; that I had not been five minutes sat upon the sopha beside her, but I had begun to form designs; and what is it but the sentiments of religion, and the persuasion they had excited in her breast, which could have check'd them as they rose up?

We are not adamant, said I, taking hold of her hand, and there is need of all restraints, till age in her own time steals in and lays them on us. But, my dear lady, said I, kissing her hand, 'tis too, too soon——

I declare I had the credit all over Paris of unperverting Madame de V——. She affirmed to Mons. D—— and the Abbé M——, that in one half-hour I had said more for revealed religion than all their Encyclopedia had said against it. I was lifted directly into Madame de V——'s *Coterie*, and she put off the epocha of deism for two years.

I remember it was in this *Coterie*, in the middle of a discourse, in which I was showing the necessity of a *first cause*, that the young Count de Faineant took me by the hand to the farthest corner of the room to tell me my *solitaire* was pinn'd too strait about my neck. It should be *plus badinant*, said the Count, looking down upon his own, but a word, Mons. Yorick, *to the wise*——

And *from the wise*, Mons. le Count, replied I, making him a bow, *is enough*.

The Count de Faineant embraced me with more ardour than ever I was embraced by mortal man.

For three weeks together, I was of every man's opinion I met. *Pardi ! ce Mons. Yorick a autant d'esprit que nous autres.—Il raisonne bien*, said another. *C'est un bon enfant*, said a third. And at this price I could have eaten and drank and been merry all the days of my life at Paris. But 'twas a dishonest *reckoning*—I grew ashamed of it. It was the gain of a slave—every sentiment of honour revolted against it. The higher I got, the more was I forced upon my *beggarly system*; the better the *Coterie*, the more children of Art. I languish'd for those of Nature: and one night, after a most vile prostitution of myself to half a dozen different people, I grew sick, went to bed, order'd La Fleur to get me horses in the morning to set out for Italy.

MARIA–MOULINES

I never felt what the distress of plenty was in any one shape till now. To travel it through the Bourbonnois, the sweetest part of France—in the hey-day of the vintage, when Nature is pouring her abundance into every one's lap, and every eye is lifted up—a journey through each step of which Music beats time to *Labour*, and all her children are rejoicing as they carry in their clusters; to pass through this with my affections flying out, and kindling at every group before me; and every one of them was pregnant with adventures.

Just Heaven! it would fill up twenty volumes—and alas! I have but a few small pages left of this to crowd it into; and half of these must be taken up with the poor Maria my friend Mr. Shandy met with near Moulines.

The story he had told of that disorder'd maid affected

188

me not a little in the reading; but when I got within the neighbourhood where she lived, it returned so strong into my mind, that I could not resist an impulse which prompted me to go half a league out of the road, to the village where her parents dwelt, to inquire after her.

'Tis going, I own, like the Knight of the Woeful Countenance, in quest of melancholy adventures; but I know not how it is, but I am never so perfectly conscious of the existence of a soul within me, as when I am entangled in them.

The old mother came to the door. Her looks told me the story before she open'd her mouth: she had lost her husband; he had died, she said, of anguish, for the loss of Maria's senses, about a month before. She had feared at first, she added, that it would have plunder'd her poor girl of what little understanding was left, but, on the contrary, it had brought her more to herself. Still she could not rest; her poor daughter, she said, crying, was wandering somewhere about the road——

Why does my pulse beat languid as I write this? and what made La Fleur, whose heart seem'd only to be turned to joy, to pass the back of his hand twice across his eyes, as the woman stood and told it? I beckoned to the postillion to turn back into the road.

When we had got within half a league of Moulines, at a little opening in the road leading to a thicket, I discovered poor Maria sitting under a poplar. She was sitting with her elbow in her lap, and her head leaning on one side within her hand; a small brook ran at the foot of the tree.

I bid the postillion go on with the chaise to Moulines and La Fleur to bespeak my supper, and that I would walk after him.

She was dress'd in white, and much as my friend described her, except that her hair hung loose, which before was twisted within a silk net. She had, superadded likewise to her jacket, a pale green ribband, which fell across her shoulder to the waist; at the end of which hung her pipe. Her goat had been as faithless as her lover: and she had got a little dog in lieu of him, which she had kept tied by a string to her girdle: as I look'd at her dog, she drew him towards her with the string. "Thou shalt not leave me, Sylvio," said she. I look'd in Maria's eyes, and saw she was thinking more of her father than of her lover or her little goat; for as she utter'd them, the tears trickled down her cheeks.

I sat down close by her; and Maria let me wipe them away as they fell, with my handkerchief. I then steep'd it in my own, and then in hers, and then in mine, and then I wip'd hers again, and as I did it, I felt such undescribable emotions within me, as I am sure could not be accounted for from any combinations of matter and motion.

I am positive I have a soul; nor can all the books with which materialists have pestered the world ever convince me to the contrary.

MARIA

When Maria had come a little to herself, I ask'd
her if she remembered a pale thin person of a man, who
had sat down betwixt her and her goat about two years
before? She said, she was unsettled much at that time,
but remember'd it upon two accounts—that ill as she
was, she saw the person pitied her; and next, that her
goat had stolen his handkerchief, and she had beat
him for the theft. She had wash'd it, she said, in the brook,
and kept it ever since in her pocket to restore it to him in
case she should ever see him again, which, she added, he
had half-promised her. As she told me this, she took the
handkerchief out of her pocket to let me see it; she had
folded it up neatly in a couple of vine-leaves, tied round
with a tendril. On opening it, I saw an S. marked in one
of the corners.

She had since that, she told me, strayed as far as Rome,
and walk'd round St. Peter's once and return'd back;
that she found her way alone across the Apennines; had
travell'd over all Lombardy without money; and through
the flinty roads of Savoy without shoes. How she had

borne it, and how she had got supported, she could not tell, but *God tempers the wind*, said Maria, to the shorn lamb.

Shorn indeed ! and to the quick, said I; and wast thou in my own land, where I have a cottage, I would take thee to it and shelter thee: thou shouldst eat of my own bread and drink of my own cup; I would be kind to thy Sylvio; in all thy weaknesses and wanderings I would seek after thee and bring thee back. When the sun went down I would say my prayers; and when I had done thou shouldst play thy evening song upon thy pipe, nor would the incense of my sacrifice be worse accepted for entering heaven along with that of a broken heart.

Nature melted within me, as I utter'd this; and Maria observing, as I took out my handkerchief, that it was steep'd too much already to be of use, would needs go wash it in the stream. And where will you dry it, Maria ? said I. I'll dry it in my bosom, said she; 'twill do me good.

And is your heart still so warm, Maria ? said I.

I touched upon the string on which hung all her sorrows. She look'd with wistful disorder for some time in my face; and then, without saying any thing, took her pipe, and play'd her service to the Virgin. The string I had touch'd ceased to vibrate: in a moment or two Maria returned to herself, let her pipe fall, and rose up.

And where are you going, Maria ? said I. She said, to Moulines. Let us go, said I, together. Maria put her arm within mine, and lengthening the string, to let the dog follow—in that order we enter'd Moulines.

MARIA-MOULINES

Tho' I hate salutations and greetings in the market-place, yet when we got into the middle of this, I stopp'd to take my last look and last farewell of Maria.

Maria, though not tall, was nevertheless of the first order of fine forms. Affliction had touch'd her looks with something that was scarce earthly—still she was feminine, and so much was there about her of all that the heart wishes, or the eye looks for in woman, that could the traces be ever worn out of her brain, and those of Eliza out of mine, she should *not only eat of my bread and drink of my own cup*, but Maria should lie in my bosom, and be unto me as a daughter.

Adieu, poor luckless maiden ! Imbibe the oil and wine which the compassion of a stranger, as he journeyeth on his way, now pours into thy wounds—the Being who has twice bruised thee can only bind them up for ever.

THE BOURBONNOIS

There was nothing from which I had painted out for myself so joyous a riot of the affections, as in this journey in the vintage, through this part of France; but pressing through this gate of sorrow to it, my sufferings have totally unfitted me: in every scene of festivity I saw Maria in the background of the piece, sitting pensive under her poplar; and I had got almost to Lyons before I was able to cast a shade across her.

Dear sensibility! source inexhausted of all that's precious in our joys, or costly in our sorrows! thou chainest thy martyr down upon his bed of straw, and 'tis thou who lift'st him up to HEAVEN. Eternal fountain of our feelings! 'tis here I trace thee, and this is thy *"divinity which stirs within me"*; not that in some sad

and sickening moments, "*my soul shrinks back upon her-self, and startles at destruction*"—mere pomp of words!
—but that I feel some generous joys and generous cares
beyond myself; all comes from thee, great, great SENSORIUM
of the world! which vibrates, if a hair of our heads but
falls upon the ground, in the remotest desert of thy
creation. Touch'd with thee, Eugenius draws my curtain
when I languish, hears my tale of symptoms, and blames
the weather for the disorder of his nerves. Thou giv'st a
portion of it sometimes to the roughest peasant who
traverses the bleakest mountains. He finds the lacerated
lamb of another's flock. This moment I beheld him leaning
with his head against his crook, with piteous inclination
looking down upon it! Oh! had I come one moment
sooner! It bleeds to death—his gentle heart bleeds with it.

Peace to thee, generous swain! I see thou walkest off
with anguish. But thy joys shall balance it, for happy is
thy cottage, and happy is the sharer of it, and happy
are the lambs which sport about you.

THE SUPPER

A shoe coming loose from the fore-foot of the thill-horse, at the beginning of the ascent of Mount Taurira, the postillion dismounted, twisted the shoe off, and put it in his pocket; as the ascent was of five or six miles, and that horse our main dependence, I made a point of having the shoe fasten'd on again, as well as we could; but the postillion had thrown away the nails, and the hammer in the chaise-box being of no great use without them, I submitted to go on.

He had not mounted half a mile higher, when coming to a flinty piece of road, the poor devil lost a second shoe, and from off his other fore-foot. I then got out of the chaise in good earnest; and seeing a house about a quarter of a mile to the left-hand, with a great deal to do I prevailed upon the postillion to turn up to it. The look of the house, and of every thing about it, as we drew nearer, soon reconciled me to the disaster. It was a little farm-house, surrounded with about twenty acres of vineyard, about as much corn, and close to the house, on one side, was a *potagerie* of an acre and a half, full of every thing which could make plenty in a French peasant's house; and on the other side was a little wood, which furnished wherewithal to dress it. It was about eight in the evening when I got to the house, so I left the postillion to manage his point as he could, and for mine, I walk'd directly into the house.

The family consisted of an old grey-headed man and his wife, with five or six sons and sons-in-law, and their several wives, and a joyous genealogy out of them.

They were all sitting down together to their lentil-soup; a large wheaten loaf was in the middle of the table; and a flaggon of wine at each end of it promised joy through the stages of the repast—'twas a feast of love.

The old man rose up to meet me, and with a respectful cordiality would have me sit down at the table. My heart was set down the moment I enter'd the room; so I sat down at once like a son of the family; and to invest myself in the character as speedily as I could, I instantly borrowed the old man's knife, and taking up the loaf, cut myself a hearty luncheon; and as I did it, I saw a testimony in every eye, not only of an honest welcome, but of a welcome mix'd with thanks that I had not seem'd to doubt it.

Was it this; or tell me, Nature, what else it was that made this morsel so sweet—and to what magic I owe it, that the draught I took of their flaggon was so delicious with it, that they remain upon my palate to this hour?

If the supper was to my taste, the grace which followed it was much more so.

THE GRACE

When supper was over, the old man gave a knock upon the table with the haft of his knife, to bid them prepare for the dance. The moment the signal was given, the women and girls ran all together into a back apartment to tie up their hair and the young men to the door to wash their faces, and change their sabots; and in three minutes every soul was ready upon a little esplanade before the house to begin. The old man and his wife came out last, and placing me betwixt them, sat down upon a sopha of turf by the door.

The old man had some fifty years ago been no mean performer upon the viole, and, at the age he was then of, touch'd it well enough for the purpose. His wife sung now-and-then a little to the tune, then intermitted, and join'd her old man again as their children and grandchildren danced before them.

It was not till the middle of the second dance, when for

some pauses in the movement wherein they all seem'd to look up, I fancied I could distinguish an elevation of spirit

different from that which is the cause or the effect of simple jollity. In a word, I thought I beheld *Religion* mixing in the dance—but as I had never seen her so engaged I should have look'd upon it now as one of the illusions of an imagination which is eternally misleading me, had not the old man, as soon as the dance ended, said that this was their constant way; and that all his life long he had made it a rule, after supper was over, to call out his family to dance and rejoice; believing, he said, that a cheerful and contented mind was the best sort of thanks to Heaven that an illiterate peasant could pay.

Or a learned prelate either, said I.

THE CASE OF DELICACY

When you have gain'd the top of Mount Taurira, you run presently down to Lyons: adieu then to all rapid movements ! 'Tis a journey of caution; and it fares better with sentiments, not to be in a hurry with them; so I contracted with a Voiturin to take his time with a couple of mules, and convey me in my own chaise safe to Turin through Savoy.

Poor, patient, quiet, honest people ! fear not: your poverty, the treasury of your simple virtues, will not be envied you by the world, nor will your vallies be invaded by it. Nature ! in the midst of thy disorders, thou art still friendly to the scantiness thou hast created; with all thy great works about thee, little hast thou left to give, either to the scythe or to the sickle; but to that little thou grantest safety and protection; and sweet are the dwellings which stand so shelter'd.

Let the way-worn traveller vent his complaints upon the sudden turns and dangers of your roads, your rocks, your precipices, the difficulties of getting up, the horrors of getting down, mountains impracticable, and cataracts, which roll down great stones from their summits, and block his road up. The peasants had been all day at work in removing a fragment of this kind between St. Michael and Madane; and by the time my Voiturin got to the place, it wanted full two hours of completing before a passage could any how be gain'd: there was nothing but to wait with patience. 'Twas a wet and tempestuous night: so that by the delay, and that together, the Voiturin found himself obliged to keep up five miles short of his stage at a little decent kind of an inn by the road-side.

I forthwith took possession of my bed-chamber, got a good fire, order'd supper; and was thanking Heaven it was no worse, when a voiture arrived with a lady in it and her servant-maid.

As there was no other bed-chamber in the house, the hostess, without much nicety, led them into mine, telling them, as she usher'd them in, that there was nobody in it but an English gentleman; that there were two good beds in it, and a closet within the room which held another. The accent in which she spoke of this third bed did not say much for it. However, she said there were three beds, and but three people, and she durst say, the gentleman would do anything to accommodate matters. I left not the lady a moment to make a conjecture about it, so instantly made a declaration that I would do any thing in my power.

As this did not amount to an absolute surrender of my bed-chamber, I still felt myself so much the proprietor, as to have a right to do the honours of it—so I desired the lady to sit down, pressed her into the warmest seat, call'd for more wood, desired the hostess to enlarge the plan of the supper, and to favour us with the very best wine.

The lady had scarce warm'd herself five minutes at the fire, before she began to turn her head back, and give a look at the beds; and the oftener she cast her eyes that way, the more they return'd perplex'd. I felt for her—and for myself; for in a few minutes, what by her looks, and the case itself, I found myself as much embarrassed as it was possible the lady could be herself.

That the beds we were to lie in were in one and the same room, was enough simply by itself to have excited all this, but the position of them, for they stood parallel, and so very close to each other, as only to allow space for a small wicker chair betwixt them, rendered the affair still more oppressive to us. They were fixed up moreover near the fire, and the projection of the chimney on one side, and a large beam which cross'd the room on the other, form'd a kind of recess for them that was no way favourable to the nicety of our sensations. If any thing could have added to it, it was that the two beds were both of them so very small, as to cut us off from every idea of the lady and the maid lying together; which in either of them, could it have been feasible, my lying beside them, though a thing not to be wish'd, yet there was nothing in it so terrible which the imagination might not have pass'd over without torment.

As for the little room within, it offer'd little or no consolation to us; 'twas a damp cold closet, with a half dismantled window-shutter, and with a window which had neither glass or oil paper in it to keep out the tempest of the night. I did not endeavour to stifle my cough when the lady gave a peep into it; so it reduced the case in course to this alternative—that the lady should sacrifice her health to her feelings, and take up with the closet herself, and abandon the bed next mine to her maid, or that the girl should take the closet, &c., &c.

The lady was a Piedmontese of about thirty, with a glow of health in her cheeks. The maid was a Lyonoise of twenty, and as brisk and lively a French girl as ever moved. There were difficulties every way—and the obstacle of the stone in the road, which brought us into the distress, great as it appeared whilst the peasants were removing it, was but a pebble to what lay in our ways now. I have only to add, that it did not lessen the weight which hung upon our spirits, that we were both too delicate to communicate what we felt to each other upon the occasion.

We sat down to supper; and had we not had more generous wine to it than a little inn in Savoy could have furnish'd, our tongues had been tied up, till necessity herself had set them at liberty, but the lady having a few bottles of Burgundy in her voiture, sent down her Fille de Chambre for a couple of them; so that by the time supper was over, and we were left alone, we felt ourselves inspired with a strength of mind sufficient to talk, at least, without reserve upon our situation. We turn'd it every way, and debated and considered it in all kinds of lights in the course of a two hours' negotiation; at the end of which the articles were settled finally betwixt us, and stipulated for in form and manner of a treaty of peace—and I believe with as much religion and good faith on both sides, as in any treaty which has yet had the honour of being handed down to posterity.

They were as follow:

First, As the right of the bed-chamber is in Monsieur, and he thinking the bed next to the fire to be the warmest, he insists upon the concession on the lady's side of taking up with it.

Granted, on the part of Madame; with a proviso: that as the curtains of that bed are of a flimsy transparent cotton, and appear likewise too scanty to draw close, that the Fille de Chambre shall fasten up the opening, either by corking pins, or needle and thread, in such manner as shall be deem'd a sufficient barrier on the side of Monsieur.

Secondly, It is required on the part of Madame, that Monsieur shall lay the whole night through in his robe de chambre.

Rejected: Inasmuch as Monsieur is not worth a robe de chambre; he having nothing in his portmanteau but six shirts and a black silk pair of breeches.

The mentioning the silk pair of breeches made an entire change of the article, for the breeches were accepted as an equivalent for the robe de chambre; and so it was stipulated and agreed upon that I should lay in my black silk breeches all night.

Thirdly, It was insisted upon, and stipulated for by the lady, that after Monsieur was got to bed, and the candle and fire extinguished, that Monsieur should not speak one single word the whole night.

Granted; provided Monsieur's saying his prayers might not be deem'd an infraction of the treaty.

There was but one point forgot in this treaty, and that was the manner in which the lady and myself should be obliged to undress and get to bed. There was one way of doing it, and that I leave to the reader to devise; protesting as I do, that if it is not the most delicate in nature, 'tis the fault of his own imagination—against which this is not my first complaint.

Now when we were got to bed, whether it was the

novelty of the situation, or what it was, I know not; but so
it was, I could not shut my eyes; I tried this side and that,
and turn'd and turn'd again, till a full hour after midnight;
when Nature and patience both wearing out, O my God!
said I.

You have broke the treaty, Monsieur, said the lady,
who had no more sleep than myself. I begg'd a thousand
pardons, but insisted it was no more than an ejaculation.
She maintain'd 'twas an entire infraction of the treaty.
I maintain'd it was provided for in the clause of the third
article.

The lady would by no means give up the point, though
she weaken'd her barrier by it; for in the warmth of the
dispute, I could hear two or three corking pins fall out of
the curtain to the ground.

Upon my word and honour, Madame, said I, stretching
my arm out of bed by way of asseveration——

(I was going to have added, that I would not have trespass'd against the remotest idea of decorum for the world)——

But the Fille de Chambre hearing there were words between us, and fearing that hostilities would ensue in course, had crept silently out of her closet, and it being totally dark, had stolen so close to our beds, that she had got herself into the narrow passage which separated them, and had advanced so far up as to be in a line betwixt her mistress and me——

So that when I stretch'd out my hand, I caught hold of the Fille de Chambre's——

A SELECTION OF
MACDONALD ILLUSTRATED CLASSICS